Sacramental Identity

Sacramental Identity

Finding Who We Are through Participation in God's Story

T. RYAN DILLON

WIPF & STOCK · Eugene, Oregon

SACRAMENTAL IDENTITY
Finding Who We Are through Participation in God's Story

Copyright © 2024 T. Ryan Dillon. All rights reserved. Except for brief quotations in critical publications or reviews, no part of this book may be reproduced in any manner without prior written permission from the publisher. Write: Permissions, Wipf and Stock Publishers, 199 W. 8th Ave., Suite 3, Eugene, OR 97401.

Wipf & Stock
An Imprint of Wipf and Stock Publishers
199 W. 8th Ave., Suite 3
Eugene, OR 97401

www.wipfandstock.com

PAPERBACK ISBN: 978-1-6667-3477-5
HARDCOVER ISBN: 978-1-6667-9098-6
EBOOK ISBN: 978-1-6667-9099-3

03/25/24

Unless otherwise indicated, all Scripture quotations are from The ESV® Bible (The Holy Bible, English Standard Version®), © 2001 by Crossway, a publishing ministry of Good News Publishers. Used by permission. All rights reserved.

Scripture quotations taken from the (NASB®) New American Standard Bible®, Copyright © 1960, 1971, 1977, 1995, 2020 by The Lockman Foundation. Used by permission. All rights reserved.

To Lanny Hubbard,
My teacher and friend.
Thank you for being someone who has "set his heart to study the law of the Lord, practice it, and teach his statutes and rules" (Ezra 7:10).

Contents

Preface ix
Acknowledgments xi
Abbreviations List xiii

PART 1 | TRACING A HISTORY — 1

1. The Identity Crisis of "Identity" — 3
2. "Personal" Identity in a "Secular Age" — 13

PART 2 | MODELS OF IDENTITY — 45

3. The Authenticity Model — 47
4. The "Identity in Christ" Model — 66

PART 3 | A SACRAMENTAL IDENTITY — 79

5. Identity in the Great Tradition — 81
6. Sacramental Identity — 101
7. Conclusion — 136

Bibliography — 141

Preface

IN 2012 TO 2013, I underwent what I can only describe as an identity crisis. I was a young college student living away from home, and all the things about myself that I felt were most important to who I was and how one might speak of me and identify me were changing. I felt lost, and I did not know what to do. I searched for answers in conversations with pastors and teachers and, of course, on the internet, hoping to find resources or books written on this from a biblical perspective. Some of these sources proved to be more helpful than others. First of all, I found no comfort in what was the stock answer from most, that my identity was "in Christ." Namely, when I asked what that meant, I received circular answers, "It means that, as a Christian, your identity is no longer in those things that you once identified with, but instead in the fact that you are in Christ." I also found no books on the topic (note: I was a young college student with average grades, so this doesn't mean that there were no books on the subject; it's just that I was not very good at finding them). I found a sermon series on identity that preached through the book of Ephesians. That gave me something, so I ran with it and decided to read the book of Ephesians twice daily. That is the origin story of the book which you hold in your hand. I found in Scripture the hope, comfort, and peace that I needed, particularly as my readings of the book of Ephesians pointed me to the church. Thus began my interest in personal identity.

The book you are holding started with many ideas and initial proposals, which I am thankful were only ever pitched to God and me. The one thing that remained constant in them all was its rootedness in the church and what God is doing in and with the body of Christ and in that place where he meets us in a unique way in word and sacrament. I also knew that in looking at identity, I wanted to seek to provide an answer to the question that I asked regarding what it means for one's identity to be "in

Christ" that didn't minimize embodiment or become a treatise on union with Christ rather than treating the initial question of personal identity. I believe this has been the death knell for theological treatises on personal identity. As will be made clear, I am not opposed to the "identity in Christ" language (I couldn't be; it is highly scriptural). I am opposed to using it as a trope or using it to accidentally (or purposefully) avoid difficult questions of embodiment, change, and time as they relate to one's identity.

I do not claim to answer all these questions or provide satisfactory answers to the questions for which I propose solutions. However, I hope that I have at least asked new questions or old questions in new ways and put forth different ways of thinking about these questions so that we can continue to move forward in our thinking about personal identity. It is always a vital topic for the church, but especially right now when so many of the questions in the overlap of church and culture are around the matters of identity. We cannot afford to do any theological anthropology not engaged with deep, thoughtful, and critical cultural exegesis. This means reading the experts but also doing the deeply pastoral work of your own cultural exegesis of the local culture in which you live and minister—which, for me, at the time of writing, is Portland, Oregon—and speaking with the local pastors of that same area.

That being said, I hope and pray that the following is helpful to any who picks up and reads it. Still, I should note that it is written more with scholars, pastors, or the slightly more academically inclined layperson who might be going through an identity crisis of their own in mind.

T. Ryan Dillon
The Holy Innocents, 2024
Beaverton, Oregon

Acknowledgments

A PROJECT LIKE THE following is always a community project. It has been made possible by so many in my life over the last decade of my academic career to this point. While the project was strengthened by the following people, any shortcomings or oversights are certainly my own.

First of all, my parents, Tim and Lori Dillon, deserve my endless thanks and praise for not only modeling what it looks like to love and live for the Lord in all that you do but for continually believing in me in times that showed no evidence of ever looking up. It could only have been out of faith in God's plans that they continued to believe in and encourage me throughout my life and initial dreams of going to seminary. Second, my sisters, Audra and Rebekah, and their husbands, Larry and Thomas, deserve great thanks. They endured tortuous rants about how ridiculous I thought the idea of education was in my teenage years, only to suffer through longer rants about all the exciting things that I was learning throughout my ten years of being in college and seminary. Thank you.

To all my Portland Bible College professors, thank you for pouring so much into me, especially Lanny and Joanne Hubbard, who have been kind, loving, and gracious throughout the years. My graduation from PBC and Western were possible only because of you and your wonderful family. To all of my Western Seminary professors, you have formed me and my thinking so much. However, I am more thankful for how you have helped me look more like Jesus by guiding me personally and modeling a life lived for Jesus. Special thanks for this project go to Drs. Ryan Lister, Todd Miles, and Patrick Schreiner, who served as supervisors and examiners during my ThM at Western Seminary, where this project originated. I would also like to think Dr. Hans Boersma who read an early version of the last two chapters and gave very helpful feedback and encouragement as I sought publication.

ACKNOWLEDGMENTS

The writing of the thesis and the subsequent book you hold in your hands could not have happened without the great encouragement and love of wonderful friends and the church community who asked questions and engaged with the topics found in these pages. I would not be who I am today without the community group that my wife and I found at AJC. You all know who you are; we have learned, fought, cried, and laughed together. But the most important thing we have done is pray together. If it was not for God's bringing us together when he did, I am horrified at the thought of where I'd be. Hakeem Bradley, Berley White, and Brandon Rude give meaning to "a friend who sticks closer than a brother" (Prov 18:24). They have read my work and pressed me on it. They have also called me out and pulled me out of dark places with the light of Christ that they carry in them. I love you guys and am thankful for who you are. Finally, this project ultimately led me to the Anglican tradition. I have had the privilege of learning under and serving Rev. Sean Flannery and the Rev. Dr. Kurtley Knight at Church of the Vine since 2021, and it has served me and my spiritual formation tremendously and, in turn, has formed this work and led me into future projects. Thank you for the conversations, prayers, shepherding, and guidance you have provided these last two years. May the Lord bless you and your families and all your kingdom work.

In its first form, this project was written to the tunes of The Tallest Man on Earth, The Japanese House, and The Chariot. This process of shaping that work into this book was fueled by Dashboard Confessional, Armor for Sleep, Bonny Light Horseman, and The Beatles; their musical accompaniment was vital to the whole process. Different writing moods called for different styles of music, and these artists really covered the whole landscape.

Lastly, but without a doubt, the most important acknowledgment goes to my beautiful wife, Amber Dillon. You have remained a constant beacon of hope in my darkest times by pointing to and helping me walk toward the light of Christ. You have loved me fiercely. You have made me laugh endlessly. And you have made me think deeply. I love you, and I will never stop "just looking at ya."

Abbreviations List

ACCS	Ancient Christian Commentary on Scripture
ACNA	The Anglican Church of North America
BCP	*The Book of Common Prayer*
CBTS	A Catholic Biblical Theology of the Sacraments
CCC	Catechism of the Catholic Church
Conf.	St. Augustine's *Confessions*
CP	Christina Rossetti, *The Complete Poems*
De Isaac	St. Ambrose's *Isaac, or The Soul*
De Laps.	St. Cyprian's *On the Fallen*
Ep.	Seneca's *Epistulae Morales ad Lucilium*
FC	The Fathers of the Church Series
Ira.	Seneca's *On Anger*
KD	Epicurus's *Principal Doctrines*
Med.	Marcus Aurelius's *Meditations*
NovT	*Novum Testamentum*
RCS	Reformation Commentary on Scripture
SSBT	Short Studies in Biblical Theology
SV	Epicurus's *Vatican Sayings*

PART 1

Tracing a History

1

The Identity Crisis of "Identity"

WITHOUT A DOUBT, THOUGHTS about one's identity are universal. This is not to say that all think about identity similarly. However, we all seem to have *a* conception of identity. The question "Who am I?" is one that we all ask at one point or another. The circumstances that bring us to such a question may vary, but we all ask it at one point or another. In 2015, both Dictionary.com and the Australian National Dictionary Centre chose *identity* as their word of the year.[1] The fact of the matter is that everything has an identity.[2] In the West, the matter of "identity politics" has pressed the matter further.[3] In Dictionary.com's article on the reasons for their 2015 choice, they cite matters of gender, sexuality, and race, as well as cultural phenomena such as Caitlyn Jenner's *Vanity Fair* cover, Rachel Dolezal's—a former NAACP

---

1. Coulmas, *Identity*, 1; Dictionary.com, "Why 'Identity' Was Dictionary.com's 2015 Word."

2. The point was driven home for me by the fact that, when I was reading Dictionary.com's article on their 2015 choice, there was an inline link to their 2021 word choice located in the words "One word has shaped this year's identity to the core." It seems that even calendar years can have an identity. (For those who are curious, the 2021 word of the year is "allyship.")

3. The terrible irony of identity politics is that it demands greater justice for those historically marginalized groups by recognizing and respecting one's differences. The presumed hope is that such an ideology would lead to greater unity despite differences; in fact, it might be said, a greater unity due to such recognition of differences. Indeed, as Coulmas notes, "Sameness and difference, this is what identity is all about" (*Identity*, 3). However, the political and ideological emphasis on such identity has only antagonized the differences and stretched them to the breaking point, exacerbating the disunity.

chapter president—presentation of herself as a black woman, and Miley Cyrus's identification as pansexual in *Elle*.[4]

That being said, the ubiquity of a term does not translate to the ubiquity of its definition. Liz McMillan, CEO of Dictionary.com, stated, "The trends that we saw linguistically all point to a larger shift in the way society thinks about identity as being more fluid"[5] and this seems to be naturally paired with a fluid meaning of 'identity' itself. And so we are left with the need to define the term. What do I mean by *identity*? Not only are such basic definitions of keywords necessary for book length treatment on the subject to which any given word symbolizes, but the definition of identity and this statement from McMillan that identity is becoming more fluid is, in many ways, the point of the following discussion. The larger questions that will loom over us all as you continue reading will be "What is identity?" "How does one and where or in what do I find or discover my identity?" "Does my identity change over time or stand firmly fixed in something that is essential to my existence?" In some ways, I hope to answer these questions in the following pages. Yet, in another way, I hope to raise new questions or come at old questions from new angles.[6] As Eccl 1:9 says, "Nothing is new under the sun," though there is still beauty under the sun and there is still much to contemplate under the sun of which the depth is inexhaustible. So what is the identity of *identity*?

The term *identity* has had its own crisis. And while there are many definitions or perhaps sub-definitions that could be offered here, I primarily want to chart out two primary understandings that will need to be introduced as a sort of definitional landscape. From here, these two definitions could be understood as two buckets into which any other definition fits. Broadly speaking, the distinction between them might easily be summed up in how certain academic disciplines speak of identity. Metaphysical conversations in the department of philosophy may largely discuss identity in one sense,

---

4. These examples all come from Dictionary.com, "Why 'Identity' Was Dictionary.com's 2015 Word."

5. McAfee, "'Identity' Is the Dictionary.com Word," §6.

6. I will never forget the description a professor of mine gave for a five-day intensive seminar on theological anthropology: "great discussions, more questions than answers, all the good stuff." Not only was that true of the class, but I think it is true of any good theological rigor and discussion I have been involved in. This is not because the participants or authors have no proposed answers—they certainly do—but they simply answer with humility, recognizing that such answers may, in fact, only ask more questions and give the ongoing discussion more vitality.

while the social sciences (particularly anthropology, sociology, and psychology) discuss identity in another. Another way, one that may be somewhat simplistic, could come from Coulmas's statement that identity is a matter of sameness and difference. On the one hand, one speaking of the "is-ness" or "nature of a human person" will focus on and say that it is the similarities that one finds in human persons that make up their identity *as* human persons. On the other hand, another person speaking of personal identity will want to focus on their differences from others and speak of that as their identity (e.g., I am a white, male, who is a theologian, musician, and coffee connoisseur).[7]

Further, another way of discussing identity, particularly in theological discourse and which we will spend more time on here, can be found in Ryan Peterson's work, who brings well-ordered categorization and makes more explicit these categories of meaning within theological anthropology by differentiating between "created" identities and "constructed" identities.[8] The former refers to those aspects of ourselves which are intrinsic to who we are as a creature made by God; this identity—what we will call identity1—is that which makes us human and is focused on ontological matters. The latter—what we will call identity2—is the identity that has been formed extrinsically by social factors, personal history, culture, etc. This is what I will be discussing here and will talk about in terms of personal identity. In theological treatises, it is the former that has been given emphasis and serious inquiry. It could be argued, in fact, that the former has largely been the whole task of theological anthropology.[9] The latter, however, is how a person might typically think about identity themselves, asking the question "Who am I?" This question is

---

7. Although, I must admit, one could quite persuasively argue that these things do very little to mark me off as different. I am quite sure that there are many who fit that exact same description, but hopefully my point is still made, no matter how "vanilla" I may be.

8. Peterson, "Created and Constructed Identities," 124–43. Peterson specifically notes created identities as "creaturely, covenantal, redeemed, and eschatological" and constructed identities as "racial, ethnic, national, religious, gender, and sexual" (124). Interestingly, Peterson seems to almost inadvertently abandon his use of these terms of distinction in the following sentence when he states, "Many of today's pressing ecclesial and ethical issues turn on assumptions about the nature and status of personal and social identities" (124.) Presumably, "personal and social identities" map onto "constructed identities" as one's nature as a redeemed person is certainly not just personal or social. That being said, the rest of his essay does specifically seek to press the importance of distinguishing these identities in these ways and doing so with clarity within theological discourse, and I think he does this admirably throughout his work.

9. This is largely due to the discipline's overall focus on humanity as made in the image of God, which is a "created identity."

of great interest and concern to people because it is an ongoing question that one must continually ask of themselves as they change over time.

Certainly, Peterson's bifurcation between identities that are "created" and "constructed" is good and has much biblical and theological grounding and force. Furthermore, his argument that "the use of identity-language in theological anthropology must be disciplined by the doctrines of God and creation and that two forms of 'identity'—created identity and constructed identity—need to be distinguished from one another" is exactly right.[10] To be sure, if identity language within theological anthropology is not grounded in the doctrine of God, then it is no longer *theological* anthropology. However, it does seem to me that Peterson's work puts a certain emphasis on created identities and, while I think there is a certain truth to such a schema, there seems to be a missing element.

It is here that I believe the work of Marc Cortez is particularly important and helpful. Cortez's work on a "Christological Anthropology" focuses equally on being a faithfully *theological* anthropology; however, he does this by grounding such discussions on the person of Christ. In his essay of the same volume, Cortez enters into dialogue with Irenaeus to argue that Jesus and our Christology "should ground our understanding of humanity." In other words, Jesus is paradigmatic for understanding humans and humanity in general.[11] Throughout the essay, he makes four important points, but it is the first that I am most interested in for our purposes here, and that is that "theological anthropology must be rooted in the embodied humanity of the incarnate Christ."[12] This claim is nothing less than startling, but it is key for balancing the nature of Peterson's arguments, which seem to prioritize "created identities" that tend to be rooted in realities that are largely detached from embodiment because our embodied selves must necessarily succumb to outside realities and therefore be constructed by them. In Cortez's larger work, *ReSourcing Theological Anthropology*, he drives his point home in remarkable ways.[13] It is to this work that we now turn.

First, his seventh of eleven theses, which he presents as guidance for moving forward in Christologically grounded anthropology, states that "Christological anthropology must pay close attention to the concrete

---

10. Peterson, "Created and Constructed Identities," 124.
11. Cortez, "Nature, Grace, and Christological Ground," 24.
12. Cortez, "Nature, Grace, and Christological Ground," 24.
13. Cortez, *ReSourcing Theological Anthropology*.

particularities of Jesus' existence."[14] That is, a Christologically grounded anthropology must be grounded in the incarnate Christ. However, Christ is not some abstract human; he was made incarnate in a human body of particularities that can be differentiated from other particularities and, therefore, result in "constructed identities." Second, Cortez does not leave this claim in the abstract but presents three examples in his final chapters. Cortez discusses ways in which our humanity is grounded in Jesus as a gendered human, a racialized person, and one who even experiences death and dying.[15] Yet, all of this entails that there is a created-ness, an *is*-ness that is inherent within these embodied particularities. Now, here is not the place to rehearse all these matters (indeed, much more will be said on this subject in a later chapter), but this should serve to illustrate the layers of difficulty in defining a term as slippery as *identity*. There are many elements that come into play and muddy the waters when it comes to neat bifurcations of "created" or "constructed" identities.

If all this was not enough, there is one further complication that relates particularly to biblically grounded, theological construals of identity. First, *identity* is a "word that does not appear in most translations of Scripture and for which there is no immediately obvious corresponding Hebrew or Greek word."[16] Though this is hardly a stable justification for ignoring an entire topic within theological anthropology, one does not have to look far to discover areas of great theological interest and import that are not based on frequent and direct mention of certain terms but rather the implications of larger frameworks and biblical discourse.[17] As we will see, this topic of identity can certainly be seen in claims made in Scripture (e.g., Gal 3:28; compare Col 3:11; Eph 1–2).[18] In fact, Klyne Snodgrass has argued exten-

---

14. Cortez, *ReSourcing Theological Anthropology*, 182.

15. These matters are covered in Cortez, *ReSourcing Theological Anthropology*, chapters 6, 7, and 8, respectively.

16. Snodgrass, "Introduction to a Hermeneutics of Identity," 4. However, as Snodgrass notes, Judith Lieu does suggest πολιτεία as an equivalent term in *Neither Jew nor Greek?*, 179. And suggests himself that ψυχή is a close equivalent to the English "identity" (Snodgrass, "Introduction," 4n6).

17. An example of this within theological anthropology would be issues of gender/transgender issues wherein the Scriptures do not themselves speak explicitly to our modern constructs and conversations around transgender issues. However, it does not mean that we cannot or should not speak to these matters from Scripture.

18. The statements made here in these portions of Scripture speak to certain aspects of personhood and the transformation that occurs in union with Christ. These truths are truths about our identity that have an impact on our self-conceptions and are there, in

sively that identity is the very message of Scripture and the ultimate goal of our faith in Christ.[19] The lack of coverage of this topic within theological anthropology has resulted in an amorphous definition and detrimental misunderstanding of this important subject. The problem with this is that "Individuals all go somewhere to take their identity";[20] that is, every day that people make claims or believe the claims of another about themselves, their identity is further formed in a certain trajectory, and the church cannot afford to stay silent in her theological discourse and treatises on the matter. Second, and very briefly, there is certainly a degree of semantic overlap between what I have called identity$_2$—or personal identity—and what is often called spiritual formation or even sanctification. Though more will be said that clarifies the overlap, it is necessary to note here that this raises more questions about the study of personal identity. Sanctification or spiritual formation is certainly a part of the identity formation for a Christian. However, while identity formation is not less than sanctification and spiritual formation, it is certainly more than this.[21]

But what of other definitions and understandings of identity and its formation, outside of the purview of theological study? It is important to look at these definitions since, within theological or biblical study, there is a necessary connection or grounded-ness within the created identity. A well-accepted understanding of identity in the second sense can be found in the *Handbook of Self and Identity*, "Identities are the traits and characteristics, social relations, roles, and social group memberships that define who one is."[22] Identities form self-concepts, which is what one thinks of when one thinks of themselves and

> This feeling of knowing oneself is based in part on an assumption of stability that is central to both everyday (lay) theories about the self and more formal (social science) theories about the self. Yet . . . the assumption of stability is belied by the malleability, context sensitivity, and dynamic construction of the self as a mental construct. Identities are not the fixed markers people assume them to be but are instead dynamically constructed in the moment.[23]

---

part, for that purpose.

19. Snodgrass, *Who God Says You Are*, 28–48.
20. Snodgrass, "Introduction," 5.
21. Furthermore, the language and meaning of "spiritual formation" are anything but clear or unanimously agreed upon by the studies' leading experts and teachers.
22. Oyserman et al., "Self, Self-Concept, and Identity," 69.
23. Oyserman et al., "Self, Self-Concept, and Identity," 69.

THE IDENTITY CRISIS OF "IDENTITY"

The fixed nature of one's identity is entirely dependent on one's social environment and context and its stability.[24] So, identity is no fixed thing; in fact, identity is no *one* thing either. A person may have *several* identities which will remain in flux throughout their life. Identity and self-concept are also seen in individualistic and autonomous terms. Self-concept is not only seen as a product of one's identity but also forms our identities. That is to say, identity formation may contain something of a circularity. Our interaction in the world around us speaks to who we are and forms self-concepts which, in turn, change the decisions we make and the ways we interact, thus informing our identity.[25]

There are important things to note on these different construals of identity. That is, in these brief surveys of different definitions and understandings of identity from both theological and psychological disciplines there are elements of continuity and discontinuity. First, any understanding of identity consists of both malleable and fixed components. A certain understanding may stress one over the other (e.g., Peterson's stress on the fixed, or "created," identity markers). However, it seems that any understanding of identity must recognize both, its malleability and its fixity. Second, the elements which make up one's identity and its formation seem to prize or center around the individual.

With these things in mind, we can now begin to discuss the aims, features, and roadmap of this work. I am interested in the strange dilemma of this dual nature of identity. How do we construct a truly theological anthropology of identity[26] that attains to the problems set forth by the fixed nature of identity and the unavoidable realities of change over time that occur through our own stories of our lived, embodied lives? My approach will focus on story or narrative. I do this because a biblically grounded theology should ultimately be grounded in the narrative of Scripture. God is telling a story of which we are characters and wherever our identity may be found—and I do hope that this book will answer that very question—it

---

24. These concepts of malleability and stability may be understood in connection with nature vs. nurture. That is, what is inherent to one's nature as human beings and ways that one is born vs. those things that are nurtured in someone throughout their life through their parents/guardians, educational background or something of the sort.

25. Oyserman et al., "Self, Self-Concept, and Identity," 70.

26. I say *"truly* theological" to nod to John Webster's call for a "theological theology." I was tempted to call it a "theological theological anthropology," but Grammarly doesn't like the repetition. For a good intro to Webster's theological methodology and project of "theological theology," see Allen, "Toward Theological Theology," 217–37.

is certainly found somewhere in that grand narrative.[27] That said, I will ultimately argue that one's identity is found in the place where our own individual stories meet and join with God's story of the world and its redemption. I will argue that the place where we can best understand and see that happening is in our participation in the sacraments. I will discuss only the sacraments of baptism, the Eucharist, and confession here. However, I would not limit the power and identity-forming nature of the other four sacraments.[28]

By way of staying story-driven in my approach and understanding of identity, and for that matter the sacraments as well, it is important that we chart out a bit of a narrative of identity itself and the way that it has been understood at different times and in different cultures. Therefore, in chapter 2, I will chart out what is really a brief narrative history of two things that I have come to find are inextricably intertwined: the history of a loss of transcendence, or what Charles Taylor calls the "immanent frame." That is, the world has closed itself off almost entirely from any belief in divine action or supernatural occurrences from a transcendent world or being. The history of this immanentization of the world, I will argue, is tied up with and plays a large part in the shifting of our understanding of identity into the amorphous, individualistic forms of self-expression and authenticity.

As I will explore in chapter 3, the "Authenticity" model of identity is a highly storied or narrative identity model that focuses entirely on the ever-changing story of the individual and the full expression of that embodied story. I will show examples of this authenticity model in different literature and give a critical appraisal of this model and its strengths and weaknesses in accomplishing the task of an identity model that answers the questions of stability and change in identity over time.

In chapter 4, I will discuss another common model of identity, which I call the "in-Christ" model. I will discuss what is the prominent way of

---

27. I am thankful here for the advice of Scot McKnight to theologians in *Five Things Biblical Scholars Wish Theologians Knew*.

28. I recognize that my language here assumes much regarding an ongoing conversation around the sacramental nature of confession and the other four "sacraments," which are not universally held to be sacraments. I offer a brief apology for my sacramental view of confession in the final chapter and my sacramental view of all reality. I hope to address the nature of the seven sacraments and those things that some call "sacramentals" in later work. However, for this work, I must assume the sacramental nature of these things and the participation metaphysics of the sacraments. For an extended discussion of these matters, see the works of Hans Boersma, *Heavenly Participation*; Davison, *Participation in God*; Davison, *Why Sacraments?*

speaking about personal identity within Christian theology. I will primarily interact with two recent monographs on personal identity, both of which focus on the "created" identity of being made in God's image and what this means for us. That is, we are primarily creatures and children of God who are known by him and made to be like him. In the same way, I will give a critical appraisal of this model and what I see as its true strengths and weaknesses in accounting for the same factors of stability and change in identity over time. It is important to note that, as I will discuss further in these two chapters, I do find both of these models to have major strengths in their understanding of identity. Indeed, the "in-Christ" model has much scriptural language to attest to its importance as a way of looking at identity. However, in the end, I find them both lacking in explanatory power and the ways in which these models recognize both stability and malleability in personal identity. Further, they both lack key components to a robust and developed narrative that would give them the full explanatory power for a person's identity.

In chapter 5, I will begin moving into a constructive model of identity found in the sacraments and their participatory nature. However, before fully proposing the sacramental identity, I travel back in time again to look at the three sacraments in the writings of three figures in the history of the church and see the ways they understood these sacraments as formative for one's identity. I will look at Saint Ambrose of Milan and his theology and liturgy of baptism, the eucharistic theology in the poetry of nineteenth-century Anglo-Catholic Christina Rossetti, and, finally, at Saint Augustine of Hippo's understanding of confession. I do this not only to establish my proposal in the tradition of the church but also because these three thinkers and writers, in particular, root their theology of these sacraments (and one's identity, for that matter) in the story of Scripture.

Finally, in chapter 6, I build out my own understanding of how the sacraments shape and stabilize one's identity in the story of God without neglecting our own individual and personal stories and the story of Christ's church. I take each sacrament in turn and seek to establish these sacraments in the narrative of God. This means that our look at these sacraments will be firmly grounded in the story of Scripture and the exegesis of that story before turning to the more theological and metaphysical aspects of the sacraments and understandings of time and participation.

As I set out to write what were the beginnings of this work in my ThM thesis in 2019 to 2020, I primarily set out to write a work on personal identity, which came out of a recognition that nothing of great theological rigor had really been written on the subject. I had undergone a time in which personal questions of identity had loomed large in my life, and I found no substantive answers to those questions. As I finished the work, it had occurred to me that I had perhaps written a work on the sacraments as much as I had a theological anthropology of personal identity. This was in large part due to a particular shift in my own identity occurring once again when my wife and I began attending an Anglican parish after both growing up in largely non-denominational churches our entire lives. Therefore, the earlier work lacked what I hope will be seen in this book as a more mature understanding of things that were merely seeds just beginning to germinate at the time. I now write as a self-conscious, albeit young, Anglican theologian who has seen the fruit of the thinking and living out of the words in these pages. That is to say, I not only believe the following to be true because I believe it is a biblically and theologically faithful way of understanding identity and the sacraments, but I have experienced the transformative and identity-forming power of the sacraments (and the liturgy for that matter, though that is for another work) in my own life. I can only hope and pray that the following pages might lead you, the reader, into your own experience of the grace of Christ's sacraments in a similar way.

2

"Personal" Identity in a "Secular Age"

THE HISTORY OF AN idea is important, and how the West has come to think about identity is essential. When I first embarked on this research in seminary, my focus had been on how we have come to believe so individualistically. I was primarily interested in the ways in which one's personal identity began to be thought of in just such a way: personal. However, as I continued reading, it became evident that the history of entrenched individualism and a loss of transcendence are intertwined. These ideas ultimately reinforce each other. The more convinced someone becomes of either of these ideas, the greater the reason to hold the other. Said differently, the loss of a sort of transcendence or a loss of a view towards any divine other leads to a belief that all one needs is his/herself. And the more one seeks autonomy, the greater the reason to let go of any transcendent, divine other who holds an intrinsic and ultimate authority over his creation.

This is the reason for the title of this chapter. I have placed the word "personal" in scare quotes to allude to the fact that it is a bit of a misnomer in relation to identity. As I will continually suggest, one's identity is never entirely personal. It is, at every point, shaped by and suggestive of a person's community and culture; they are identified by this or that descriptor or self-expression insofar as they identify with this or that social group. In other words, as I suggested above, one's story speaks to their identity, and no person's story is told in isolation. In fact, even if one were to live their whole life entirely alone, their story would be told and identity formed around the questions of their relationship to the lack of others in their life,

PART 1 | TRACING A HISTORY

thus still entirely formed by their community and its anomalous absence. Furthermore, all of this is not to mention that all people are created by God and created in his image, and therefore their identity is wrapped up in this Creator/creature distinction, this I/Thou relation.

In the same vein, the quotes around "secular age" nod to Charles Taylor's magnum opus, *A Secular Age*, which tells the "story . . . of secularization in the modern West."[1] These are the two histories that I seek to survey here. While my survey of the loss of transcendence within the final pages of this chapter is heavily indebted to Taylor,[2] my study of the former within those same pages is indebted to the brilliant sibling works of Carl Trueman, *The Rise and Triumph of the Modern Self* and *Strange New World*. What I seek to add to the discussion of these works is their connections with one another. Although Trueman is in some conversation with the work of Taylor, he ultimately sets out on his journey with the primary sources of Descartes, Rousseau, Marx, Nietzsche, and Freud. What I seek to show through the conclusions of this chapter is that the by-product of Trueman's history, "the modern self," is something that ultimately begins even sooner than he charts it and that the modern self of Trueman's work is finally a by-product of Taylor's historical narrative of the buffered self.

Such a survey will necessarily be selective. An exhaustive history would require a book-length treatment (as Taylor and Trueman have proven). However, by the end of the chapter, I hope to have shown that the ideas are not coincidentally related at points throughout history but genuinely weave in and out of each other.

But why embark on such a detour in the first place? In many ways, it would be enough to chart some modern models of identity and self-conception, appraise them, and then propose my model of a sacramental identity. However, before moving on to those primary current models, I believe this history will not only set them in their proper context but will also show how the "immanent frame"[3] and the resulting individualism undergird the problematic aspects of these models of identity. This will better set the foundation for my proposal that it is a sacramental universe and participation in the particular sacraments of Christ and his church that

---

1. Taylor, *Secular Age*, ix.

2. This indebtedness to Taylor is served by much help from the work of Boersma, *Heavenly Participation*.

3. Taylor, *Secular Age*.

form and hold up our identity and offer a remedy to the ongoing and unending search for one's true self.

Secondly, as I've mentioned, identities are narratively indexed. Regardless of the model of identity taken, a person cannot avoid the relation of their own story and the stories they are a part of with their identity. It might be said that the baseline of any identity model is a narrative identity model, and the difference is what narrative is primary or how that narrative is seen and understood in its identity-making force, and my proposal is no exception. That being said, it will be necessary to trace important moments in the story of us all and our philosophical and theological heritage. This intellectual heritage has had a tremendous impact on the identity of us all and how we have come to think about that identity even if, and perhaps, especially when, we are unaware of that intellectual heritage. Prevailing philosophies and theologies of the age do much in shaping the culture which raises and forms those who live in it.[4]

Because this is a Christian/biblical and theological account of identity, the journey will start with the world of the Old Testament (OT) and the understanding of identity in the ancient Near East (ANE).[5] From there, we will survey how hellenization began shaping how one understood their identity. We will focus mainly on prevailing Greek philosophical schools and their individualistic shape. However, as I hope to show, individualism is merely supposed here, as such a shape was unable to form fully without the loss of transcendence that would come later. And it is that loss of transcendence or the building of the "immanent frame" to which we will then turn as we explore the Middle Ages through to Modernity and Post-Modernity. I will engage heavily with Charles Taylor and Hans Boersma to show how this period begins what Boersma describes as the fraying and eventual tearing of the sacramental tapestry.

---

4. This is true even of those who act in intellectual rebellion to their heritage and seek to propose a new philosophy or theology to prevail over the current, and often thought, outmoded or outdated philosophy or theology. Such rebellion is not so much a striking out on their own or independence from the resented heritage but is more dependent upon that heritage than ever before, as it needs the resented heritage to make sense of such new proposals. That is, it needs the narrative of what has come before to create conceptual space for what is to come. More will be said on this later in regard to individuality and authenticity.

5. One might accuse me here of anachronism, a crime of which I am guilty. However, while the term *identity* may be anachronistic, the idea of self-conceptions and what forms or influences those self-conceptions is not, and that is what will be discussed in this section on the ANE.

With this in mind, it is to the world of the ANE that we now turn.

SELF-CONCEPTION IN THE THOUGHT OF THE ANCIENT NEAR EAST

In 1911 with the publication of H. W. Robinson's *The Christian Doctrine of Man*[6] the relation between the individual and the community became a major interest of investigations of the anthropology of the ancient Near East, particularly within the socio-religious context of Israel. In his work, Robinson proposed an idea of "corporate personality" from English law. The term refers to a level of conflation between individual and corporation. Robinson used the term to describe the Hebrew understanding of the individual as he saw it, in which "men dealt . . . not on the basis of the single life which consciousness binds together for each of us, but as members of a tribe, a clan or a family . . . the idea that the sin of one (e.g., Achan) can properly be visited on the group to which he belongs, and into which his own personality, so to speak, extends."[7]

Since that work the idea of corporate personality or solidarity has become the primary way in which many have understood some of the challenging language of the OT about Israel and the individual people of the nation. For instance, Robinson's example in the quote above is the story of Achan in Josh 7. In the story we see an occurrence of corporate responsibility for the sinful action of an individual. Another example is that of the seemingly corporate use of the first-person singular in the Psalms, such as 44:5–9 where the psalmist moves seamlessly and interchangeably between the first person singular and plural.

Robinson's contributions have not gone on without their fair share of critiques, however. There are some who believe that Robinson has pressed the conception too far and deny that the socio-religious context of Israel and the ANE had any conception of the individual at all. J. W. Rogerson fears this is an attempt "to fit OT texts into simplistic categories." He believes that while it is wrong, and perhaps naive, to simply assume that an ancient culture operates with the same understanding of the relationship between the individual and society as modern society, "it is equally wrong to suppose that the OT can only be understood by

---

6. Robinson, *Christian Doctrine of Man*.
7. Robinson, *Christian Doctrine of Man*, 8.

positing a special Hebrew mentality, radically different from that of modern Westerners."[8] In the same article Rogerson uses the same example as Robinson and shows how there is still much individual responsibility indicated in the story of Achan.

Despite these criticisms, there is much to be lauded about Robinson's contributions in understanding OT conceptions of anthropology and identity. In fact, the concept's leading detractor, Rogerson, has even said:

> It remains likely that Israelites saw society as an aggregate of groups rather than as a collection of individuals, that in worship the king could embody the aspirations of the whole community, and that individuals in worship or prayer could feel that their experiences were those of the whole group.[9]

The tension that Rogerson seeks to hold is that, while Israelites saw society in such ways and did place a large emphasis on group identity, these did not derive "from some kind of primitive mentality."[10] Thus, in the story of Achan, we see elements of guilt and shame of the individual and society. Only Achan and his family are killed, yet there are repercussions for all of Israel (e.g., the defeat at Ai [7:1–9]). Indeed, it is said that all of Israel has transgressed their covenant with the Lord and it is clear that elements of shame would inevitably have fallen on the tribe of Judah, clan of the Zerahites, and the line of Zabdi (Josh 7:17–18).

However, my point here is not to reconstruct debates regarding "corporate personality" in the OT and ANE societies. My point here is to show that OT scholarship has—though without consensus on the exact structure or methodology by which to interpret such facts—recognized a corporate element in these societies' understanding of the self and its formation. Indeed, in commenting on Josh 7:1, Walton, Matthews, and Chavalas state, "In the ancient Near East a person found his or her identity within the group. Integration and interdependence were important values, and the group was bound together as a unit. . . . this corporate responsibility was also a result of the covenant relationship that Israel had with the Lord."[11] Thus people in the ANE thought of their identity in terms of their relation to the other, and Israel did this in terms of their relation to the Lord or the divine other as well as to the societal other.

---

8. Rogerson, "Corporate Personality," 1:1157.
9. Rogerson, "Anthropology and the Old Testament," 25.
10. McConville, *Being Human in God's World*, 64.
11. Walton et al., *IVP Bible Background Commentary*, 218.

In fact, a major theme of the OT is seeing how Israel's relationship to God shapes how they relate to the other (both Israel and the nations) and vice versa. Therefore, as we continue to work through the understanding of the self according to the Israelites in the OT, it is important to understand that many of these things are shaped by their larger and more foundational relationship to God. That is, much of their more corporate or social sense of identity is founded and dependent on their belief in a transcendent God that gives meaning and *telos* to everything they do. Therefore, it is here that J. Gordon McConville's OT anthropology becomes quite helpful. In his book, he dedicates chapters to discussing the influence of place, memory, and work. These three categories are the main ways in which one can begin to understand the Old Testament's anthropology and the means by which Israel and other ANE societies understood the formation of who they were. These three categories are important to our understanding of identity because of the Israelite's conception of the self and how they highlight their corporate understanding of identity formation.

Place

Place is inescapable when considering the factors of one's identity. Humans, by their very nature of being embodied, are always geographically and historically located, and these particulars inevitably inform who we are and how we interpret the world around us.[12] However, place is a particularly important category for our understanding of the OT and the Israelites' conception of themselves as individuals and as a people. From the first page of the Bible, we can see that the overall story is just as much about הָאָרֶץ ("earth," "land," "ground") as it is אָדָם ("mankind").

Indeed, mankind's placement in the story is intrinsically connected to the earth. Not only is mankind created from the ground, but it is created for an immediately stated purpose of having dominion over the earth, and all that inhabits it (Gen 1:26–28; 2:7, 15). More will be said about this later in our discussion of work, but for now, it is important to see how the narrative sets us up to understand the importance of place within the biblical

---

12. Place and culture are tied in the way that place has an effect on our culture's influences. We can see this in our ways of speaking about "southern" hospitality or charm (something that I missed when moving from southern Kansas to California). On a larger scale, one of the more commonly noted differences in place and culture is the difference between the West's guilt/innocence culture vs. the East's honor/shame culture. See Tennent, *Theology in the Context of World Christianity*, 77–101.

narrative. We see the storyline continue where Adam and Eve are evicted from the garden in Gen 3, in the stories of Noah and of the tower of Babel that feature land as a major plot-thickening character (Gen 6–11), and finally in the call of Abraham to leave behind his current place to a land that the Lord would show him (Gen 12). The relationship between Abraham and his descendants and the land to which God would call him becomes the underlying plot of the entire Hebrew Bible. McConville writes, "The Old Testament might be described as the record of Israel's long and tumultuous engagement with land."[13] That is, ultimately, Israel's story and understanding of themselves are intricately connected with their placedness,[14] where they are from, and where they are going. The Israelites found place as formative to their identity. It was their being connected with the external world and its inhabitants through cohabitation with others in the world who share this same placedness. We can see it particularly at the end of Joshua after the land allotments in which their placedness was connected to their familial or tribal lineage, which certainly left an indelible mark on their identity (Josh 13–21).[15]

Furthermore, before we move on to discussing memory, I want to reiterate not only the importance of *where* we are for our identity but also *when* we are. That is, our place in time matters for how we are formed and the things that impact our understanding of ourselves. A large-scale version of this point is what this chapter is setting out to do; to locate ourselves within our own historical context to understand how our understanding of identity has changed and what some of the intellectual and cultural culprits might be for that shift. However, a smaller scale of this is true as well. It doesn't require changes between large epochs for our chronological place to have an impact on who we are. Even contemporaries can be entirely different in their understanding of themselves and the world around them. This is what we are picking up on when we recognize the differences between

13. McConville, *Being Human in God's World*, 99.

14. I use "placedness" to refer to that fact and quality of being located and situated in a particular place.

15. What I am referring to here is the way in which, after these land allotments to the families or tribes of Israel, these tribes became intricately connected to a particular place. These places developed a particular culture and contained geological particularities which further developed and formed the identity of their inhabitants. So, a tribe's location will lend towards their being more militarized due to their vulnerability to foreign invaders or experts in a particular trade due to the land's fertile soil. See for instance Josh 20 and the cities of refuge being located in the land of particular tribes, which would inevitably affect the inhabitants and their formation as mediators.

the Millennial generation and what we call Gen Z. Therefore, thinking again about the people of Israel, we can seek to be perceptive of the difference between the generation who were enslaved and crossed the Red Sea before entering into the time of wandering in the wilderness and the second generation, who never experienced this liberating miracle of God but were simply born into this wilderness. What differences do such things make in one's understanding of who they are? Such differences are a matter of memory. And it is to that point that we now turn.

Memory

Following closely behind the matter of place and its formation of societal and individual identity, McConville introduces memory. In line with his statement above regarding the OT's emphasis on Israel's relationship with land and place, he states:

> The entire Old Testament might be considered a work of memory. At its core are the decisive formative events of creation, exodus, and Mosaic covenant, and much of the Old Testament can be understood as a layered testimony both to those events and to the ways in which they have been remembered.[16]

The kind of memory being spoken of here is often referred to as "social" or "corporate" or "collective" memory. It is a memory that is lived and embodied rather than called to mind or recalled via inquiry into the past. It might be better understood as a cultural or collective habit such as liturgy.[17] This is particularly important to keep in mind in light of the fact that not all the people had a core personal memory of these events. So they are shaped by these events in different ways. Their own stories shape them and it is this story that they bring with them to their own re-telling and living out of the collective story.

The importance of and way of carrying forth corporate memory for Israel is best seen in their calendar year, which was assembled around celebrating feasts and festivals. The most prominent of these is Passover. The regulations of the first Passover are given to us in Exod 12, and later celebrations are depicted in Leviticus and Deuteronomy as "a pilgrimage

---

16. McConville, *Being Human in God's World*, 110.

17. For more on this sort of memory or "liturgy" and its importance for the formation of identity, see the work of Smith, *Imagining the Kingdom*; and Johnson, *Human Rites*.

festival in which the people were required to bring the appropriate offerings to the central (Jerusalem) sanctuary."[18] Other festivals include *Sukkot* (Feast of Booths, see Lev 23:33–44), *Shavuot* (Feast of Weeks, see Deut 16:9–12), and *Rosh Hashanah* (Feast of Trumpets, see Lev 23:23–25). These annual festivals are celebrated together in memory of what God has done for them as his people.

It is not difficult to see how memory impacts not only the group or society's identity but also that of the individuals within that group. Jan Assmann states that "an individual who grew up in perfect solitude should have no memory at all. Memory will be accrued to humans in the course of their socialization. Although it is always the individual who 'has' recollections, they are collectively shaped."[19] As such, it would have dramatic effects on the identity of an individual and further shows the necessity of community and corporate memory in the formation of an individual's identity2. The distinction between "history" and "memory" made by Yosef Yerushalmi is instructive here. Yerushalmi states that "history" contemplates facts at a distance, whereas "memory draws from the past a series of situations into which one could somehow be existentially drawn."[20] The distinction made here helps us better understand how memory might shape one's identity. Drawing on Yerushalmi's work, Miroslav Volf states about Jews and Christians, "Take away the memories of the Exodus and Passion, and you will have excised the pulsating heart that energizes and directs their actions and forms their hopes."[21]

Further, G. K. Beale, in *We Become What We Worship*,[22] shows through canonical and intertextual exegesis that the Bible understands spiritual habit as formative for one's identity. The main thrust of Beale's argument is that God and the biblical authors begin to describe idolaters in the same way as the idols themselves: with eyes and ears but without sight or hearing. Beale summarizes his comments on Isa 6 showing that those expressions used to describe Israel are for the purpose of emphasizing the fact they would be judged in the same way as their idols and says, "This pronouncement of judgment also includes the idea that the idolaters had begun to

---

18. Chalmers, *Exploring the Religion of Ancient Israel*, 121.

19. Assmann, "Cultural Memory," 163.

20. Yerushalmi, *Zakhor*, 44. See my section below on the sacraments, sacramental time, and their stabilizing effects on identity.

21. Volf, *End of Memory*, 97.

22. Beale, *We Become What We Worship*.

resemble their idols: they had become as spiritually blind and deaf as their idols. . . . the idols that Israel believed were alive were in reality lifeless and objects of cursing, and the nation had become the same."[23] Beale concludes, "The biblical-theological principle expressed by Isaiah 6 is that we resemble what we revere, either for ruin or restoration."[24] It is easy to take for granted the ways in which our corporate memory or liturgy shape us until we see the ways in which we are shaped by the destruction of those rituals. Beale's study shows that side of ritual shaping in Israel's life, brilliantly. It was as Israel lost sight of their history, failed in the practice of corporate memory, and were in exile that they become like their idols.

It seems that the prescribed liturgy for the Israelites was as much about the Lord's desire for the people to continually remember who they were, individually, as part of Israel, the covenant people of Yahweh, as it was to give proper worship and glorification of the one true God. While these may be seen as two sides of the same coin, it is worth reflecting on the neglected side of identity formation. For, we can see throughout Israel's history how it was at times when they abandoned their cultural memory or began to incorporate the collective habits of other nations that Israel seemed to forget their identity. What follows is Israel is then described in terms akin to that of lifeless idols.

What this means for our own tracing of identity is that the formation and conception of one's self should be conceived of in yet another communal or corporate category for Israel. They found their identities as marked by the corporate memory of the community of which they were a part. A criticism may be raised here regarding whether this might truly be conceived of in terms of an individual's identity formation or as society's identity formation. However, one should not be so quick to make such distinctions. Although cultural memory is, in fact, a communal rather than individual experience, it does take place within and through embodied individuals. It is also the means by which individuals are incorporated into the social body and what Charles Taylor calls a society's "social imaginary."[25] Further, the lived, corporate memory of feast, festivals, and holy days assumed a world enchanted with the transcendent. The people of Israel took

---

23. Beale, *We Become What We Worship*, 63.

24. Beale, *We Become What We Worship*, 64.

25. "In talking of our self-understanding, I am particularly concerned with what I will call our 'social imaginary', that is, the way that we collectively imagine, even pre-theoretically, our social life in the contemporary Western world" (Taylor, *Secular Age*, 146).

for granted that time wrapped back around itself in some divine way. The feasts were a memory of times past, but they also participated in the events of divine action that had taken place and were, in some ways, always taking place.

Lastly, this liturgical calendar of the Israelites is closely tied to the seasons and the land. Times of growth and new life and times of dormancy, times of rest and of toiling over ripe harvests. To an agricultural society and people, this amounts to a calendar of work and vocation. This subject of work, vocation, and *telos* will be the last in this portion of our historical journey.

Work

Finally, in the same way that the language of memory can be rather misleading due to cultural shifts and misreading, work has certain connotations to hearers today. What is meant by work is not necessarily labor or one's job; rather it speaks to one's vocation or overall *telos*. Individuals within Israel and the ANE were teleologically oriented and focused. That is, they were led by that purpose for which they believed they were created. Here, McConville makes much of the relation between work and creativity/beauty and what it means to be in the image of God. However, for our purposes here, I will simply focus on that which the Hebrew Bible speaks about regarding the purpose of mankind.

The understanding of the Israelites' belief about their ultimate end and purpose and the source of this understanding can be found on the first pages of the Hebrew Bible. The Israelites believed their ultimate purpose was to serve Yahweh and live in obedience to their covenant with him; to subdue and have dominion over the earth (Gen 1:26–28).[26] Despite their regular disobedience to the covenant, they still believed that their purpose, their *telos*, was to fulfill that commission given to the first man and woman and was recapitulated through the covenant with Noah (Gen 8:15–17; 9:7), Abraham (Gen 12:1–3; 15:1–5), Moses (Exod 19:3–6), and David (2 Sam 7:1–17). In all of these covenants—which God made with the leaders who were to stand as representative heads for all of God's people—a command

---

26. John H. Walton connects the dots well between the *imago Dei* and these commands in his commentary, *Genesis*, 130–32. "While the image of God defines a role for humanity (vice-regents for God), the blessing indicates the functions that people will have as a result of the role to which they were created."

and promise is made that resembles that of the one made to Adam and Eve in Gen 1–2. God's plan for his people to be fruitful, multiply, subdue and have dominion over the earth would not return void (Isa 55:11).

The concept is, in some ways, both continuous and discontinuous with the understanding of other ANE societies. When we look at the Babylonian creation myth, "The Enuma Elish," we find that humans were made for "service of the gods."[27] In yet another ancient creation text, the Sumerian "Enki and Ninmah" we see several humans being created by Ninmah, each with their own defect of sorts that are "counterbalanced" by Enki.[28] However, the means by which Enki counterbalances these fates is by placing them in different services to the king. The similarities and differences here are clear. Whereas Genesis sees mankind as having a close relationship with God and as having dominion over the rest of creation via the authority that was bestowed upon mankind, the Babylonian and Sumerian texts pictured mankind more as the brutish slaves of the king or gods.

The purpose of serving the gods becomes clearer when we look at the ANE law texts and rituals. John H. Walton and J. Harvey Walton show how mankind's relationship with the gods relied on what is called the Great Symbiosis.[29] That is, the gods created mankind to serve them and provide for them their needs and necessities, such as food and places of worship. However, if mankind were to have the means to meet these needs, they would require the service of the gods to provide rain for agricultural success, safety from natural disasters, and other such occurrences. That is, the relationship between the gods and mankind and their understanding of themselves was based on this created reality of codependence between the gods and mankind.[30]

The codependence did not end there. A natural codependence is created among mankind in this relation to the gods. We see that the way in which each individual played out their role in service to the gods was indeed different, though it seems that each person saw their purpose as ultimately found in that purpose of mankind as a whole: to serve the gods. The concept is not easily grasped by a society marked by individual autonomy and service of the self and its desires. Nevertheless, the fact that this is how ANE societies saw individual roles can further be seen in how they saw

---

27. Heidel, *Babylonian Genesis*, tablet 6.33–34.
28. Black et al., "Enki and Ninmah," lines 52–61.
29. Walton and Walton, *Lost World of the Torah*.
30. Walton and Walton, *Lost World of the Torah*, 65–69.

their role in the provision for their household (usually made up of three to four generations) and clans. That is, each individual could not technically speak of even possessing their own labor or rights in the family; those were possessed by the *paterfamilias*. This is because each individual in the household did not view themselves as their own but as one of a collective whole who lived for the service and wellbeing of the larger unit.[31]

The similarities and dissimilarities between the Great Symbiosis of the ANE and Israel's covenantally defined relationship with God are vast. As Walton and Walton state, "Everything looks much the same from outside observance, but make no mistake—everything is different."[32] In Israel, they state, "humans display God's glory and enhance his reputation rather than providing for his needs."[33] Therefore, in both, a close relationship is shared between god(s) and humans, and, in both, human work and vocation are representative of that relationship. However, the stark difference is that in Israel, this vocation is tied to their ultimate *telos* of displaying God's glory and bearing his image.

Conclusion

After having briefly surveyed the understanding of identity in ANE cultures, particularly that of Israel, we learned that their conceptions of identity and the way it is formed were all in corporate or communal categories. We also discovered that these things were greatly tied up in their understanding of the transcendent and their relationship to God and divine action. They recognized the importance of place, corporate memory, and vocation, all of which they saw as bringing them into greater unity with one another and with God. These important aspects of one's life also shaped who they were as individuals of that community. Thus, it is important to note that I am not arguing that they had some primitive anthropology that had no room for the individual. On the contrary, in each of these categories can be seen a formulation of the individual and their role in the flourishing of the community in which they were a part and which they saw as a part of them. However, though Israel and other ANE societies did have thorough conceptions of the individual, there was no concept of an isolated individuality apart from their communities.

    31. Di Vito, "Old Testament Anthropology," 217–38.
    32. Walton and Walton, *Lost World of the Torah*, 81.
    33. Walton and Walton, *Lost World of the Torah*, 81.

PART 1 | TRACING A HISTORY

A HELLENIZED IDENTITY: IDENTITY IN HELLENISTIC PHILOSOPHY

We now move into another epoch and culture to survey their conception of the self and how one's identity in the second sense is formed. Here we will survey how hellenization began to shape the ways one understood their identity. The differences that emerge in the Hellenistic age do so from the rise of Greek philosophies that began to dominate the way that people understood the world and their place in it. Hellenism is important to survey as it is commonly linked with a culture of individualism. While many of the philosophical schools of the culture and time period place a larger emphasis on the individual than that of ANE societies, there remained, as we will see, an understanding that the communities of which one was a part largely regulated the way that one existed in the world and how the self was formed. That is, the only way for one to live out the tenets of their philosophy was to live fully immersed in the world and the communities around them.

In my section here, I will examine two dominant philosophical schools that arose during the Hellenistic period and their primary teachers to show how they viewed one's place in the world and communities around them and the impact the thinking had on their identity and its formation. My reason for examining these two particular schools of thought is due to the common understanding surrounding them and their focus on the individual. However, while the teachers pressed the matter of the individual, the view that Hellenistic philosophy resulted in an autonomous and individualistic understanding of identity should be seen as primarily indefensible in light of other basic tenets of their teaching. Furthermore, the background for the development of these modes of thought are important to understand. As will be seen, they resulted as a response to major cultural shifts around them. The shift from the Hellenic age (800–323 BC) to the Hellenistic age (323–31 BC) sees a change from the *polis* to the *cosmopolis*. That is, the social and political realm moved from the city-state to a world civilization. Thus, "the Greek people had to find their way in a world that was much bigger, more complex, more chaotic, and more threatening to their security and way of life."[34]

---

34. Bartholomew and Goheen, *Christian Philosophy*, 55.

Stoicism

The first of the schools we will review is Stoicism, founded by Zeno of Citium (335–263 BC). Stoicism's goal was the happiness, peace, and serenity of the human in spite of difficult circumstances. Stoicism defines happiness in terms of wisdom, which is "conforming oneself to the providential and rational order found in the universe."[35] The Stoics adopted a fatalistic attitude and therefore sought to fall in line with the natural order of the world and their fate.[36] As such, it did not mean that the Stoics were passive. Again, the goal was to act in true wisdom by adapting oneself freely to the providential outcome of the cosmos.

It is Stoicism's fatalistic outlook on the world and its view of virtue as freely adapting oneself to the natural order that has led many to understand stoicism as a highly individualistic, though hardly autonomous, view of the self. Such an understanding is why Terence Paige can say in his brief survey of stoic thought that "the ideal Stoic life was a highly individualistic, self-centered pursuit of 'virtue' in complete independence from any external supports."[37] In line with that statement, Philip Esler engages a long standing conversation regarding the similarities and differences between Paul's epistles and Stoic philosophy and concludes that the rather individualistic thinking of the Stoics is one of the greatest divergences in Paul's thought, calling it "radically different."[38]

However, are these claims, regarding Stoicism as "individualistic," "self-centered," and "independent," defensible? It would seem that upon close reading the Stoics, though they have conceptions of the individual and what might be called "personal" identity, those conceptions are still within a larger view of the social world. That is, their larger goal was to find their individual selves in the midst of the expanding world.[39] Again, the importance of recognizing this point is to see how modern a thought and understanding it is to think about the formation of identity2 in an individualistic vacuum whereby the formation and expression of the self turn back on one another and inform each other. Further, the shift toward an

---

35. Bartholomew and Goheen, *Christian Philosophy*, 55.
36. Frame, *History of Western Philosophy and Theology*, 77–78.
37. Paige, "Philosophy," 715.
38. Esler, "Paul and Stoicism," 124.
39. See again the Bartholomew and Goheen quote above in n34.

internal look for identity comes as society shifts away from beliefs in the transcendent, as I will show at the end of the chapter.

Let us take a look at a metaphor which was popular among the Stoics. In answering a question posed to him, Seneca answers, "All that you behold, that which comprises both god and man, is one—we are the parts of one great body."⁴⁰ The body metaphor, as the one Paul uses in referring to the church (Rom 12:4-5; 1 Cor 12:12-21), was used in a way that shows how "they considered human society to be a universal brotherhood."⁴¹ Seneca expands on the idea elsewhere, saying:

> What if the hands should desire to harm the feet, or the eyes the hands? As all the members of the body are in harmony one with another because it is to the advantage of the whole that the individual members be unharmed, so mankind should spare the individual man, because all are born for a life of fellowship, and society can be kept unharmed only by the mutual protection and love of its parts.⁴²

It was not only Seneca, however, who spoke of mankind's universal bond in that manner. Marcus Aurelius also spoke of individuals as members of the universal body. He writes, "The idea of this will come home to you more if you say to yourself: 'I am a member (μέλος) of the system made up of reasonable beings.' If, however, by the change of one letter, you call yourself a part (μέρος), you do not yet love men from your heart; well-doing is not yet a joy to you for its own sake; you are still doing it as a bare duty, not yet as though doing good to yourself."⁴³ These quotations show that while, as Esler and Paige argue, Stoicism marks the small beginnings of individualist thinking and ethics, the larger category of the individual was seen as a part of the collective whole of humanity. As Thorsteinsson says, "Central to Stoic ethics was the notion that, since all men have a share in the divine and universal λόγος, all men by nature are equal and have moral obligations to each other."⁴⁴

Another Stoic philosopher who wrote much on the relation of the individual and community was Epictetus. Much of his writing could quite easily be understood as a radical individualism. In book 2 of *Discourses* he

---

40. Seneca, *Ep.* 95.51–52.
41. Frame, *History of Western Philosophy and Theology*, 77.
42. Seneca, *Ira.* 2.31.7.
43. Thorsteinsson, "Paul and Roman Stoicism," 151n38, citing *Med.* 7.13.
44. Thorsteinsson, "Paul and Roman Stoicism," 152.

speaks of what the good life is and contains. That is, one finds true happiness (εὐδαιμονία) in a "desire that is always achievable, the certainty of avoiding what is undesired, choosing what is appropriate, a thoughtful plan, a carefully considered agreement."[45] This short statement gets at what is Epictetus's overall point that happiness is found or dictated by external circumstances or those things that are outside of our control. Put another way,

> people can only be absolutely sure that they will find happiness if they center their moral purpose on themselves and their own mental states, since everything else lies outside of their powers. The goal of happiness—the goal of Epictetus's entire philosophical system, which is synonymous with virtue—can be secured in no other way than through the effort of the individual on his or her own.[46]

It is hard to get much more individualistic than that. However, this is not the whole story of Epictetus. As Dunson notes, for Epictetus, the individual is not at odds with the community, and such a focus does not take away from a focus on social responsibility.[47] This is because, as Epictetus continues, he shows how these two things—a focus on our own self-interest and on our community—can be held hand in hand. Although he maintains his ethic of self-interest as the source of happiness and the good life throughout his lecture "On Friendship" in 2.22, he states quite clearly that "the upshot is that if you identify self-interest with piety, honesty, country, parents and friends, then they are all secure. But separate them, and friends, family, country and morality itself all come to nothing, outweighed by self-interest."[48] Therefore, it is not that this sort of self-interested individualism denies others a place in one's search for the good life and attainment of true happiness; it simply takes a shift of focus or perspective on how we view others and their place in our lives.

Certainly, there is a marked difference between the Stoic ethic of Epictetus here and, as we will see in a later chapter, the Christian ethic of the apostle Paul. However, yet again, the "radical difference" that Esler maintains here, may be a bit of an overstatement. There is a shift in the way in which Paul centers the community over the self, which is contrary

---

45. Dunson, "All for One and One for All," 62, citing *Discourses* 2.8.29.
46. Dunson, "All for One and One for All," 63.
47. Dunson, "All for One and One for All," 63.
48. Epictetus, *Discourses* 2.22.18.

to Epictetus's centering of self-interest. However, both maintain a place in their ethic for the two poles.

Summarizing my look at Stoicism and its understanding of the relation between the individual and the corporate, it is important that we make explicit how it informs the Stoic view of forming one's identity in the second sense. One's understanding of their identity is intimately connected to the ways in which she views her place in the world. While the Stoics may have held a view that found their goal in personal happiness and peace through all of life, they fundamentally understood themselves as a member of the universal family or body of mankind. They hoped not only for their own pleasure and happiness but that of all others as well. Though it may have been from self-interest, it shows that they understood the formation and identity of the self in terms of the corporate rather than autonomous individualism. So, in terms of the larger project here, we discover that while Stoicism marks a turn towards perhaps a greater degree of selfishness, it is the larger framework and belief in each individual's intrinsic connectedness to all others that shaped one's ultimate identity.

Epicureanism

A philosophical school of thought established by Epicurus (341–270 BC), Epicureanism had a goal that, at first blush, seems rather similar to that of Stoicism: seeking pleasure and happiness. However, whereas the Stoics found this in adaptation to the fatalistic outcomes of the cosmos, the Epicureans sought physical pleasure and pleasures of the mind. Epicurus stressed some level of moderation and did not believe that one should over-indulge due to the suffering that could come as a result. While the goal of Epicureanism clearly emphasizes the individual, as does their sense of justice,[49] an emphasis is still largely placed on the community.

One particular instantiation of this corporate principle is found in the Epicurean view of friendship. Though their primary goal was to seek pleasure and happiness, they believed such could not be found alone. In fact, Epicurus believed that friendship was the greatest of all things which brought happiness. Cicero famously wrote of Epicureanism and the beliefs of its founder in *On Moral Ends*, saying:

---

49. O'Keefe, *Epicureanism*, 139–40.

There remains a topic that is absolutely essential to this discussion, and that is friendship. Your view is that if pleasure is the highest good then there is no room for friendship. But Epicurus' view is that of all the things which wisdom procures to enable us to live happily, there is none greater, richer or sweeter than friendship.[50]

A letter from Seneca reveals the same thing about Epicurus:

> You desire to know whether Epicurus is right in one of his letters in criticizing those who maintain that the wise man is content with himself and therefore needs no friend.... The difference here between the Epicurean and our own school is this: our wise man feels his troubles but overcomes them, while their wise man does not even feel them. We share with them the belief that the wise man is content with himself. Nevertheless, self-sufficient though he is, he still desires a friend, a neighbour, a companion.... To come back to the question, the wise man, self-sufficient as he is, still desires to have a friend if only for the purpose of practising friendship and ensuring that those talents are not idle. Not, as Epicurus put it in the same letter, "for the purpose of having someone to come and sit beside his bed when he is ill or come to his rescue when he is hard up or thrown into chains," but so that on the contrary he may have someone by whose sickbed he himself may sit or whom he may himself release when that person is held prisoner by hostile hands.[51]

Tim O'Keefe confirms this of Epicurus and his philosophy when he says, "Epicurus praises friendship in extravagant terms, calling it an 'immortal good,' which 'dances round the world announcing to us all that we should wake to blessedness.' This is because friendship is by far the greatest thing for making our whole life blessed (KD 27). Knowing that we can count on our friends to help us out in times of need allows us to face the future fearlessly."[52] The highest good that one can have is a friend.

However, that being said, it is important to recognize that there is a metaphysical shift that can be seen in Epicureanism. More will be discussed on the metaphysical shift in the next two sections, but it is worth noting here that Epicurus held to a more atomistic view of things, "On this view, everything that exists is made up of atoms, tiny bits of matter that have always existed and are indestructible.... The perceived qualities of ordinary

---

50. Cicero, *On Moral Ends*, 1.65.
51. Seneca, *Letters from a Stoic*, Letter IX, 47–49.
52. O'Keefe, *Epicureanism*, 147.

objects are all explained by the properties of the underlying atoms."[53] We can see how such an atomism might lead to a sort of detachment from a view that anything of our life here has any import for anything beyond us and our own pleasures. Indeed, much of Epicurus's questions were around the fear of death and what happens after one dies, which he believed was a matter of ceasing to exist and thus was nothing to fear. That being said, such understandings of the world were not full abandonment of transcendentalism towards atheism. Rather, they were the first moves toward what Charles Taylor calls "the buffered self." Epicurus "does not deny the existence of a god or gods; if there are such beings they too will be material in nature. What he does maintain is that the natural world is not controlled by gods; it is the product of mindless, mechanical causes. It was not created by the gods, and the gods have no interest in what happens on earth and no power to control events. There is no grand purpose or teleology in nature."[54]

So, while Epicureanism is not as individualistic because of its hedonism, as some might think, it does mark a shift toward a more naturalistic framework or immanentization that cuts the people off from a larger *telos* wherein people are a part of something bigger than just themselves. As I have mentioned above, I believe these two things go hand in hand. We will now look more at this immanentization over the course of the next two sections.

Conclusion

I have sought to give an overview of the Hellenistic age in order to trace the views of the self and its formation during this period. To demonstrate, I traced two popular philosophical schools and their ways of understanding the concept of identity in the second sense. The purpose of choosing Stoicism and Epicureanism was that they have been seen as more individualistic and autonomous schools of thought. I have sought to show that such a view is not so clear when one reads the primary teachers of these schools and their ethics.

Though one may argue that the beginnings of individualistic and autonomous modes of thought are found here in the Hellenistic age, we cannot see a major paradigmatic shift in society's view of identity as a whole.[55]

---

53. Evans, *History of Western Philosophy*, 96–97.

54. Evans, *History of Western Philosophy*, 97.

55. See Luther H. Martin's brilliant work on the problem with this generalization of

In fact, work has been done on the Hellenistic period as a whole to discover how much societies relied largely on the past and their collective/cultural memory for identity construction.[56]

Further, one reason that such a radical individualism is unable to be maintained within these philosophies is their retaining of beliefs in the transcendent. These philosophies still held to universal truths that upheld an interconnectedness of all things as the warp and woof of their philosophical world. However, as was shown, a shift was beginning in Epicurus's views, as he held to more atomistic understandings of the world and its relation to the transcendent. As we will come to see, their world was still a porous one; disenchantment had not yet fully set in.

THE POROUS SELF TO THE BUFFERED SELF: IDENTITY FROM THE MIDDLE AGES THROUGH MODERNITY

The Middle Ages (fifth c.–fifteenth c.)[57] is no small era and to truly survey the long and rather tumultuous time could very well be a project of its own. Therefore, throughout my section here, I will speak generally of the Middle Ages as a whole and trace out larger ideas and views on identity throughout the Early, High, and Late Middle Ages. The following section finally identifies the shift toward individualistic ways of thinking about identity and its formation as the world becomes disenchanted and the self is "buffered." Whereas the previous sections have focused on the ways in which societies and philosophical schools thought about identity, my final section will focus on what caused the shift from past ways of thinking to modern thought on the formation of the self. That is the shift of viewing identity more socially with views toward both God (as the transcendent other) and what I have called the societal other, to individual ways of thinking and viewing identity as more "personal" or "psychological," thus leading to what has

---

individualism in "Anti-Individualistic Ideology of Hellenistic Culture," 117–40.

56. For a survey of the literature here see: Martin, "Anti-Individualistic Ideology of Hellenistic Culture." See also Assmann, *Cultural Memory and Early Civilization*, 39–42 and 53–106 in particular.

57. It should be noted here that the reason for such a large gap in our timeline is because in part 3 we will explore the understanding of identity in the NT and among the early church fathers as a part of my primary proposal. Therefore, rather than working through those things here before addressing them later in chapter 4, I have chosen to move forward to the Middle Ages.

been called "expressive individualism." Such a focus on the shift in our intellectual history will lead us to the purposes of the next chapters, in which we will focus on two particular ways in which our individualistic thinking has played out in different models of identity formation.

The following sections do this, particularly by looking at the ways in which the church viewed the sacrament of the Lord's Supper and a sacramental ontology in general. This will allow for an easier shift into our final section, where we will particularly look at the sacraments, but it also speaks greatly to the dramatic shifts in thinking towards more inward or psychological turns to understand the world and our place in it. This will help us bridge the gap as we look at what is called "expressive individualism."

A Porous World

The major theme that will be explored here is the incredibly religious nature of the Middle Ages. After the decriminalization of Christianity through the Edict of Milan (AD 313) came the rise and development of Christian theology and society. In addition, the invasion of the Germanic peoples throughout the Roman Empire led to "a new era, in which the Roman Empire was no longer the glue that held civilization together. The maintenance of Western culture and civilization fell to the church."[58] It is also important to note that these invasions came not at the hands of pagans, but rather by Arian Christians who had been previously reached with the Christian gospel.[59] Therefore, though we might expect foreign invasion to come with a major shift in the religious culture, we instead see more of the Arian heresy coming in, which had only recently waned in majority popularity around AD 381.

The reason for my introduction to the religious context of the Middle Ages is for the sake of showing how society at the time was what Charles Taylor calls "porous."[60] The "porous self" is the language that Taylor uses to speak of the understanding that society had about their world being "enchanted," a world inhabited and—one might even say, at times, manipulated—by spirits, demons, and higher or transcendent forces. As stated above, the Middle Ages were a time in which a belief in God in general, but

---

58. Frame, *History of Western Philosophy and Theology*, 123.

59. See Ferguson, *Church History, Volume One*, 286–305 for an overview of the conversion history of these tribes and their migrations at the turn of the period.

60. Taylor, *Secular Age*, 35.

Christianity in particular was largely assumed. In fact, few other options were on offer societally. The church and the empire were so intertwined in the West and so held each other together that Christianity and its inherent view of the supernatural were largely assumed.

For our purposes, in such an "enchanted" world, it is difficult to maintain ideas of individualism, autonomy, or any view of that self that turns inward. It was understood that whatever or wherever one's identity or self might be found, it wasn't simply found in the self and authentic self-expression. Taylor states, "Things and agencies which are clearly extra-human could alter or shape our spiritual and emotional condition, and not just our physical state (and hence mediately our spiritual or emotional condition), but both together in one act. These agencies didn't simply operate from outside the 'mind', they helped to constitute us emotionally and spiritually."[61] That is to say, these "things and agencies" helped to constitute and form our whole selves and changed the way we understood the self and its formation. Taylor cites other ways in which an enchanted world and porous self alter the structures of society, such as different understandings of time and the ordering of society in classes of the elite and the masses.[62]

What Taylor calls the "medieval imaginary" goes further than merely believing in some spiritual great beyond that engages with our own world. In this imaginary, our natural world was seen as a cosmological sign pointing toward something supranatural. Therefore, our own realities, earthly *poleis*, and kingdoms were something of a Platonic existence that pointed to higher realities, i.e., their true form. It is on these greater truths, according to this imaginary, that our world finds its foundation for existence. Therefore, the world we live in is "open and vulnerable, not closed and *self-sufficient.*"[63] Thinking in line with the Platonic worldview—or what Hans Boersma calls "sacramental ontology"—means that authenticity and expressive individualism cannot be the sole fount of our identity, as this sort of individualistic narrative is only half the story since these realities point to higher realities; sharing a sacramental relationship our "selves" are the *signum* to some greater *res*.

The theologians of the Middle Ages referred to the "porous world" in these terms of sacramentality. Their sacramentality or "openness" to God's participation in our material reality can be seen in how they understood

---

61. Taylor, *Secular Age*, 40.
62. See Taylor, *Secular Age*, 54–61, 80–84, respectively.
63. Smith, *How (Not) to Be Secular*, 27 (emphasis added).

the elements of the Lord's Supper. The belief in the real presence of Christ's flesh and blood in the bread and cup is an indication that this period of time understood the world in the ways mentioned by Taylor above. In 1070, Lanfranc of Bec insisted that,

> On the one hand, there is the sacrament; on the other, there is the "thing of the sacrament." The "thing" (or the "reality") of the sacrament is the body of Christ. . . . [A]s the apostle Andrew says, while the bits of [Christ's] flesh are really eaten and his blood is really drunk, he himself nevertheless continues in his totality, living in the heavens at the right hand of the Father until such time as when all will be restored.[64]

Therefore, what we see here is an understanding that the material world truly participates (albeit mysteriously), with greater spiritual realities. Paschasius Radbertus wrote in 844 something quite similar, "A sacrament is something which is passed down to us in any divine celebration as a pledge of salvation, when what is done visibly achieves something very different and holy inwardly." In Platonic language, both of these writers understood the earthly elements of the Eucharist to participate in the forms or ideals of a greater reality. Radbertus continues, "We feed upon and drink the sacrament of the body and blood . . . so that, nourished by it, we may be made one in Christ, who sustains us this way so that we may be made ready for immortal and eternal things."[65] To these theologians of the Middle Ages, the world is porous or sacramental and participates with our Creator's higher realities as a foretaste of what is to come.

Autonomy and individualism have no oxygen in a world set within a porous world. Individualistic ways of thinking rely on a view of self-sufficiency, an ability to close oneself off from the world or worlds around them. In the end, Taylor is looking at all of these indelible marks of, particularly, the Early and High Middle Ages[66] as elements that did not lend themselves toward living individually. Taylor writes, "Living in the enchanted, porous world of ancestors was inherently living socially. It was not just that the spiritual forces which impinged on me often emanated from people around me . . . Much more fundamental, these forces often impinged on us as a

---

64. Cited in McGrath, *Christian Theology Reader*, 298.
65. Cited in McGrath, *Christian Theology Reader*, 295.
66. Taylor sees the Late Middle Ages, moving into the time of the Reformation and the Modern period, as the turn towards "disenchantment" and the buffering of the self.

society, and were defended against by us as a society."[67] Social living was not just one of living in relation to God, but also the societal other. People related closely with all others as inhabitants of the enchanted world and who, necessarily so, sought to offer the demanded and deserved worship, reverence, and devotion to God/the gods.

However, as we will see, seeking to reform this understanding of the world and how it played itself out into the castes of society led to the modern period and what Taylor calls the "secular age."[68] It is this secular turn that led to an anthropocentric worldview and to individual and autonomous views of the self.[69] As we begin our final section here, we will continue to engage Taylor and his look toward the turn to the modern period and how it led to the "age of authenticity."[70]

Two-Tiered Religion

The world as it was seen in the Middle Ages—an enchanted or, in other words, vulnerable world—created a two-tiered religion. There were the clerical elite, moving at higher speeds toward religious perfection, and the lowly laypersons, those whose spiritual or devotional practices were perfunctory at best.[71] Taylor notes the dissatisfaction with this system that came in the Late Middle Ages:

> What I'm calling "Reform" here expressed a profound dissatisfaction with the hierarchical equilibrium between lay life and the renunciative vocations. In one way, this was quite understandable. This equilibrium involved accepting that masses of people were not going to live up to the demands of perfection. They were being "carried," in a sense, by the perfect. And there is something in this that runs against the very spirit of the Christian faith.[72]

In the place of dissatisfaction, you can handle it in two different ways: you can reach down to the lower "tier" and help them up or speed them along, or you can lower the standard entirely, making it easier for them to

---

67. Taylor, *Secular Age*, 42.
68. Taylor, *Secular Age*, 42.
69. Taylor, *Secular Age*, 18–19.
70. A key theme of both Taylor, *Sources of the Self*, and Taylor, *Ethics of Authenticity*.
71. Taylor, *Secular Age*, 61–63.
72. Taylor, *Secular Age*, 61–62.

catch up.[73] However, it seems, Taylor suggests, that the former strategy of helping others meet higher expectations and thus raising the bar higher is what led others to grasp onto the latter method of letting go of the expectations of the lower tier. The latter tactic is expressed in a buffered, anthropocentric view of the world. While such a suggestion has not gone entirely unchallenged, it does help us see the complexity of the "two-tiered" nature of the religious culture of the time and how some were challenging the system and attempting to reform it.

Transcendence, Immanence, and the Sacraments

The final pieces of Taylor's telling of the beginning of modernity—that is, those intellectual shifts which began to turn around the massive ship of other-oriented views of the self—involve ideas of sacramentality and the effects that the theological principle had on views of transcendence and immanence. Though the Protestant Reformation is certainly not entirely to blame for the shift to modernity, Taylor does use some of the conversations of that period as a case study in what was happening on a larger scale during the Late Middle Ages.

A case in point are the conversations regarding the sacraments. Leading into the Early Middle Ages, discussions on the high sacramentality of the Lord's Supper began to emerge regarding a change of substance in the bread and the cup to being the Lord's actual body and blood. Originally presented by Paschasius Radbertus in his *On the Body and Blood of the Lord*, it would ignite a controversy that would not soon fade.[74] Though many would challenge the views of Radbertus, his view would ultimately hold sway. In fact, in the eleventh century it would come to a head when another objector, Berengar of Tours, would eventually be forced to renounce his objections.[75] A high sacramental view of the Eucharist is fitting of the "enchanted" view of the Middle Ages. However, the Magisterial Reformers sought to challenge ideas within the faith that might place any weight of salvation on human efforts. Transubstantiation was one such way that they believed the transference of grace was being subjected to the action of man. In a high view, grace is imbued into elements of the world which are

---

73. Smith, *How (Not) to Be Secular*, 37.

74. See Allison, *Historical Theology*, 641–42, for a summary of this controversy and its interlocutors.

75. See both Allison, *Historical Theology*, 643; and Mathison, "Lord's Supper," 644–46.

at the behest of human endeavor to receive. Taylor states, "The power of God doesn't operate through various 'sacramentals,' or locations of sacred power which we can draw on. These are seen to be something which we can control, and hence blasphemous."[76]

In the end, the world was stripped of all the other-worldly enchantment of the "good" kind. Meanwhile, the world was still seen as enchanted, even if in a lesser sense, but now only by that kind which was bad. This meant that protection from the negative, other-worldly power could only be found in ourselves. It should be noted that this is not the entirety of the move toward exclusive humanism and individualistic accounts of the self; however, it is what makes the move possible. Many other elements, religious and political, helped to make the shift possible as well. However, the overview given thus far should suffice in properly setting up certain elements of the theological legacy we have inherited that have led to our ways of thinking about identity.

Descartes and Locke

Before moving to that place and time where the most evident instantiation of autonomous and individualist thinking can be found, I want to briefly reiterate what I think Taylor tries to show throughout his account of secularism. That is, ultimately, such a largely accepted idea now inundated into people's frame of thought is difficult to trace throughout intellectual history. The turn of a ship is done slowly and just a few degrees at a time. Therefore, to trace such a turn and pinpoint the decisive move is nearly impossible. What we will see here then is not *the* decisive moment in a turn toward the immanent frame and thus an inward turn toward the self, but is rather a degree in the intellectual turn, which is but one of many moments that were large and decisive in their own way. They are then stitched together with other similar moments and mark the even larger turning point.

In the same way that the Reformation marked decisive moments in intellectual history that made the "secular age" possible, so too did René Descartes (1596–1650) and his writings. Descartes was committed to

---

76. Taylor, *Secular Age*, 79. Note that while I agree with the ways in which this story played out in favor of the secular age and more importantly for our purposes—exclusive humanism, I do not think that the purposes of the reformers were mistaken. I take it that the rhetorical force necessary to see the needed shifts in the religious structures, particularly within Catholicism at the time, was enough to create paradigm shifting momentum that was not easily stopped.

autonomous scientific reasoning. His most famous philosophical saying, which was first published in its Latin form, "Cogito, ergo sum," in his *Principles of Philosophy* in 1644, has led to what James K. A. Smith calls "thinking thing-ism" which simply assumes that the center of a human person is the mind.[77] My reason for mentioning this here is that such thinking is a massive intellectual shift toward individualistic thinking because the proof of one's existence and identity1 can be found entirely within the individual self. Aside from any philosophical debates that may deservedly stem from this point, it marks the inward move toward the self.

When the answer to the doubt that plagued Descartes—the context from which this statement comes—occurs in light of the narrative that we have just heard from Taylor, we can see this in a new light. Trevin Wax states, "Once faith is no longer axiomatic, reason and science often rush in as the objective referee in all sorts of disputes, which has led to a split between facts and values."[78] In other words, the self-sufficiency of man in the disenchanted world is already beginning to emerge. It is the reason of man that provides the answers to our most existential doubts.

On the heels of Descartes's overall project comes an important philosophical figure. John Locke (1632–1704) was a large contributor to individualism and the Enlightenment. Descartes may not be the decisive moment in the history of individualism; however, he had a large impact on Locke's thinking. In fact, an early biography of Locke notes that it was the writings of Descartes that first ignited the desire to study philosophy in Locke.[79] The two disagreed in many ways. However, it should be noted that it was Descartes's way of thinking on the matters discussed above that led to Locke's individualistic musings.

Though Locke's version of individualism is a bit different than that of the kind which we are focusing on, it is certainly one of those aforementioned moments stitched into the fabric of such thinking. Locke's individualism is a part of his political philosophy, where he "based government on the natural rights of the individual and on the social contract."[80] Stated differently, individualism is ontological in essence. An individual is naturally and ontologically prior to a society which is dependent on the collection of individuals. Therefore, the government of society should seek to serve

77. Smith, *You Are What You Love*, 3–4.
78. Wax, *Eschatological Discipleship*, 112.
79. Thilly, "Locke's Relation to Descartes," 597n1.
80. Bartholomew and Goheen, *Christian Philosophy*, 126.

the individual. Yet, at the same time, the individual's involvement in such government and society is to "maximize their own self-interest."[81]

The Enlightenment

Having traced some of the philosophical stepping stones, we are now more prepared to discuss Enlightenment philosophy, which "prioritized the individual as the basic arbiter of truth."[82] There are many key contributors to the Enlightenment and its overall project, and each figure brought something unique to the philosophical round table. Citing Peter Gay, Wax states it was "'a dialectical struggle for autonomy' in which they sought to assimilate their Christian and pagan inheritances and then become independent of them."[83]

Nowhere is this seen more clearly than in Immanuel Kant (1724–1804), with whom "the high point of Enlightenment philosophy was reached."[84] In response to the question "what is Enlightenment?" Kant answered:

> Enlightenment is man's leaving his self-caused immaturity. Immaturity is the incapacity to use one's intelligence without the guidance of another. Such immaturity is self-caused if it is not caused by lack of intelligence, but by lack of determination and courage to use one's intelligence without being guided by another. *Sapere Aude!* Have the courage to use your own intelligence! is therefore the motto of the enlightenment.[85]

The motto of the Enlightenment maps onto Taylor's definition of secularity perfectly. Now, by 1784, a buffered and autonomous/sufficient self is no longer just possible; it is a sign of maturity and true progress.

What is particularly remarkable and destructive about Kant's answer to the question of enlightenment is his focus on religion. At the end of his essay, Kant restates the first sentence of his definition with the addendum, "primarily *in matters of religion*."[86] Kant states that we are not presently in an enlightened age, but in an age of enlightenment where "venerable

---

81. Bellah et al., *Habits of the Heart*, 143.
82. Noble, *Disruptive Witness*, 41.
83. Wax, *Eschatological Discipleship*, 103, citing, Gay, *Enlightenment*, xi.
84. Bartholomew and Goheen, *Christian Philosophy*, 152.
85. Kant, "What Is Enlightenment?," 132.
86. Kant, "What Is Enlightenment?," 138–39.

clergymen could, regardless of their official duty, set forth their opinions and views even though they differ from the accepted doctrine here and there."[87] Such religious enlightenment is important because "immaturity in matters of religion is not only most noxious but also most dishonorable."[88] The obvious danger with such religious enlightenment lies in where we draw the line on who our guide is in receiving doctrine. Disagreements may be had on the role of the church and tradition in doctrinal authority, but insofar as Scripture is understood as the "norming norm," then we can confidently speak of the church and her guidance as the instrument of God's guidance in our thinking. Thus, an enlightenment that rids us of the guidance of the "true light" (John 1:9) is the actual intellectual immaturity.

What we have here is Kant's turn toward the self as the norming norm. His turn effectively seals the demise of a world that truly participates with God. In order for true progress to occur, we must rid ourselves of such external influences. To do so is to mature and be shaped not by others but by yourself. To do so is to be authentic.

Conclusion

We now come to the conclusion not only of the section but also of our historical survey. We've traced how societies and individuals have come to formulate ideas about the self and the formation of identity. Remarkably, what we've seen is that individualistic/autonomous formulations were not something that came about until the turn to the modern period. These monumental changes came as the result of philosophical, theological, and even political paradigm shifts. Furthermore, the turn came slowly and through gradual movements, one degree at a time. "Western civilization slowly shifted the locus of our hope from a transcendent source in God, who forms us, to finding it deep within ourselves."[89]

And that is the key. A severing from the divine and transcendent other detaches our ties to all others. We have created a buffer (i.e., denial) from the one thing outside of ourselves which gives lasting meaning and unites us to all others. It is now every man for himself. True progress, in fact, is having the courage to know without the help of another. One natural way of proving that we are doing just that is to hold beliefs that are different from

---

87. Kant, "What Is Enlightenment?," 138.
88. Kant, "What Is Enlightenment?," 139.
89. Noble, *Disruptive Witness*, 36.

all others. Noble is right when he says that "what is truly important to us is not only or primarily our beliefs but how they affect our identity. Identity formation becomes the central concern, and our beliefs are just another way we articulate that identity."[90] Therefore, it doesn't matter if our beliefs are contradictory; we are likely not even thinking of the congruency of our beliefs; the doctrinal hodgepodge is seen as more of an intellectual snowflake, unique in its own way and constructed without the help of another.

Taylor calls it the Age of Authenticity. Smith defines it as an "age in which spirituality is deinstitutionalized and is understood primarily as an expression of 'what speaks to me.'"[91] The idea of authenticity goes beyond spirituality, though, at least on the surface. Though the root is spiritual in the disenchantment of society, authenticity can be summed up now in the post-modern mantra to "live" or "speak your truth." To fail at either of those is to fail at being who I am, to fail at being human, and to give short shrift to the formation of my identity. In the turn I have charted throughout this chapter, we can see that increasingly our concerns have turned, along with our gaze, from the upward to the inward. And this is the problem for which I seek to offer a solution. Our thoughts about and search for our identity have been turned entirely inward, and as a response, Christians have, at times, turned entirely upward to the neglect of the inward—we can become "so heavenly minded that we are no earthly good." However, neither the wholly inward nor wholly upward gaze sees the full picture. The enchanted world or sacramental ontology of the Great Tradition recognized this. As I will argue in part 3, the Scriptures and the nature of the church and her sacraments teach us that the created matter and inward concerns of our embodiment and individual particularities participate in the upward concerns and realities of eternity.[92] More on this in the final chapter. That final point brings us to the next part, where I will explore the two primary models or ways of thinking about identity and its formation and examine their strengths and weaknesses.

---

90. Noble, *Disruptive Witness*, 38.

91. Smith, *How (Not) to Be Secular*, 140.

92. I am thankful to my priest, the Rev. Dr. Kurtley Knight, for his wonderful sermon preached on the twenty-second Sunday after Pentecost, 2022, where he helped me find the words read in the previous paragraph. Further, our conversations around the sacraments and formation have been invaluable as I write this manuscript.

PART 1 | TRACING A HISTORY

PART 2

Models of Identity

HAVING TRACED A HISTORY of the ways in which different societies and civilizations thought of identity and its formation, we arrived at the modern period and, with it, the dawn of individualism, authenticity, and the loss of transcendence or the sacramental ontology. Here we will continue to look at these ideas by examining the ways in which they have affected our current formulations of identity. In so doing, I will work through the primary tenets of each before concluding with an examination of their strengths and weaknesses.

In chapter 3, I will examine that mode which I began to outline at the close of the last chapter. The view, which might be called "Authenticity" or "Self-Representation," is the quintessential model of identity in the world today. It is individualistic in that one's identity is relative to those ways in which they define themselves and choose to represent themselves. Such a view is what it means to live authentically. Chapter 4 will then examine that which I will call the "in Christ" model. The origin of which, as I take it, is a response to our Age of Authenticity and those who have searched for themselves in the first model and either felt that they returned empty-handed or feel as though they no longer want to be defined by those things which once were so representative of who they were. The Christian response is typically that one's identity is no longer found in those particularities of their personhood but is rather found "in Christ."[1]

---

1. See Rosner, *Known by God*; *How to Find Yourself*; and Snodgrass, *Who God Says You Are*.

As I will show, both are important to a robust theology of personal identity. However, on their own, I find them lacking much explanatory power. Authenticity without the bedrock of the Christian confession of our union with Christ and its transformative power leaves us blowing in the wind, our identity unstable. The "in-Christ" identity model, it will be seen, tends to dissolve all personal narrative included in the embodied elements of our identity at worst and, at best, lacks sufficient explanatory power for what truly happens to one's embodied identity in light of our regeneration and union with Christ.

3

The Authenticity Model

AUTHENTICITY IS THE DEFINING model of identity in the secular age and our move to exclusive humanism. The emphasis on our particular individuality that describes this is the most natural result of the eruption of varying options, modes of belief, and ways of finding meaning in the secular age. This is what Charles Taylor calls "the nova effect."[1] Interestingly, Richard Lints also taps into this strange effect from a different angle, though he does not cite Taylor. He states, "One of the fundamental changes in modern consciousness is the movement from fate to choice. The power of our tools creates so many more choices than could have been conceived by any earlier civilization. The vast array of things possible now through our technological innovations makes it appear that an individual has unlimited power and unlimited choices. We are not bound by the fates of history any longer."[2] Lints goes on to note that these technological choices we have now are only a minuscule sample of the choices on offer today, many of which are more internal choices related to lifestyle, religion, and morals.[3] "The more choices, the more reflection. The individual who reflects becomes more conscious of himself. He turns his attention from the objectively

---

1. See his extended section on this phenomenon in Taylor, *Secular Age*, 299–313. Though, James K. A. Smith has a wonderfully succinct definition, "The explosion of different options ('third ways') for belief and meaning in a secular age, produced by the concurrent '*cross pressures*' of our history—as well as the concurrent pressure of *immanentization* and (at least echoes of) transcendence" (Smith, *How (Not) To Be Secular*, 142 [emphasis original]).

2. Lints, *Identity and Idolatry*, 160.

3. Lints, *Identity and Idolatry*, 160.

given outside world to his own subjectivity.... The hegemony of truth itself comes under severe scrutiny."[4] One's beliefs are more concerned with the expression of their own identity and choice than the coherent construction of such beliefs and how these guide us through life and the world. This is one of the ways by which we protect ourselves from transcendent beliefs, finding meaning and purpose within ourselves and the immanent frame. "We are buffered selves, protected behind a barrier of individual choice,"[5] and that primary choice is who we are and how we will live that out and represent ourselves authentically.

One way this can be expressed is that identity is narratively indexed; our life and all that has happened to us form our identity and make us who we are in the present: "We are our stories."[6] This is how we represent ourselves, through telling a narrative of individual choices made along the way. We live our story, and we live to tell our story in order to express our identity. As I've stated earlier, this is, on one level, fine and true. Our stories are necessarily part of who we are; they form us. However, with the "cutting of the sacramental tapestry"[7] or the construction of "the immanent frame,"[8] this becomes exclusive humanism at its finest; meaning and purpose can now be found without any necessary turn toward the transcendent; they are found solely within the self.

In this chapter, I will explore what this understanding of identity looks like. I will start by looking at recent explorations of what has come to be known as "expressive individualism" and in what ways this understanding of identity has come to be viewed as living authentically. I will look not only at Christian thinkers looking in on this view from the outside but also at where society expresses or touts this idea.

It will also be essential to look at different instantiations of authenticity by looking at how people represent themselves "authentically" as they express their identity through their stories. That is, where can we see this idea playing itself out? This understanding of identity takes place in many different related categories. However, I will focus on just two: disability studies and studies of sexuality and gender as aspects of one's story that are said to represent one's identity authentically. I will look at these areas

---

4. Lints, *Identity and Idolatry*, 161.
5. Noble, *Disruptive Witness*, 37.
6. Jacobson, "We Are Our Stories," 124.
7. Boersma, *Heavenly Participation*, 68–83.
8. Taylor, *Secular Age*.

from both confessional and non-confessional spaces. This means that the emphasis on authenticity or their weight to "expressive individualism" will differ. However, I have chosen to engage with each of these authors due to their engagement with these ideas in the particular category to show what it can look like when an idea is no longer just an area of academic interest for the sake of discussion but impacts the way one speaks about themselves or lives their life.

EXPRESSIVE INDIVIDUALISM

A term and idea that has seen a rise in usage and scholarly discussion is "expressive individualism" (EI). Robert N. Bellah coined the term in the book *Habits of the Heart*: "Expressive Individualism holds that each person has a unique core of feeling and intuition that should unfold or be expressed if individuality is to be realized."[9] Since then, Charles Taylor has discussed EI extensively throughout his book *A Secular Age*. From there, many within Evangelicalism have discussed EI, particularly with a point to critique and warn of the dangers of such thinking. My reason for including a section on EI here at the beginning of a chapter on what I call the authenticity model is because of the ways in which EI and authenticity overlap in thinking about identity. Indeed, Charles Taylor, in discussing what others call EI, describes it in the following way:

> Each one of us has his/her own way of realizing our humanity, that it is important to find and live out one's own, as against surrendering to conformity with a model imposed on us from outside, by society or the previous generation, or religious or political authority.[10]

It is evident how this description overlaps with Bellah's definition of EI; however, Taylor calls this the "culture of authenticity." Thus, our following discussion on the authenticity model is my foray into the discussion of EI which is important to note in light of the recent increase in literature surrounding EI.

In the midst of this recent explosion of literature on EI, Carl Trueman's sibling volumes stand out as particularly helpful in mapping out key thinkers and shifts in ideas, which led to society being inundated with this

---

9. Bellah et al., *Habits of the Heart*, 333–34.
10. Taylor, *Secular Age*, 475.

PART 2 | MODELS OF IDENTITY

understanding of identity. I have sought to give such a historical overview in the previous chapter with a particular look at the connection between our loss of a particular sacramental ontology and the rise of individualism, so I do not wish to repeat that work here. However, it is worth noting the difference in ways that Trueman has charted the history of EI from a different vantage point, and those interested in learning more are urged to review both of Trueman's works on the matter.

One thing that Trueman has sought to do, which pushes back against past attempts at charting similar histories, is show that EI did not simply arise out of the sexual revolution of the 1960s alone; it goes back farther than that. Trueman connects this rise to a few particular moves in thinking about the self: (1) the psychologized self in René Descartes (1596–1650) furthered by Jean-Jacques Rousseau (1712–78) and the Romantics, (2) the politicized self in Karl Marx (1818–83) and Friedrich Nietzsche (1844–1900), and then finally, (3) the sexualized self in Sigmund Freud (1856–1939).[11] One might think it hard to believe that these thinkers have had such an influence on society when they have likely only been read by so few, broadly speaking. However, this is the importance of Charles Taylor's thinking on social imaginaries, which we have briefly mentioned earlier, but is worth filling out more here. I quote Taylor, again, at length:

> I speak of "imaginary" (i) because I'm talking about the way ordinary people "imagine" their social surroundings, and this is often not expressed in theoretical terms, it is carried in images, stories, legends, etc. But it is also the case that (ii) theory is often the possession of a small minority, whereas what is interesting in the social imaginary is that it is shared by large groups of people, if not the whole society. Which leads to a third difference: (iii) the social imaginary is that common understanding which makes possible common practices, and a widely shared sense of legitimacy.[12]

Taylor's "social imaginary" helps us understand how the philosophy and writings of these thinkers have come to change the way society thinks and understands the world around us, even at an unconscious level.

Finally, before moving into examples of how we see the authenticity model of identity specifically play out, I want to give something of a fuller synthesis of my ideas on the connection between the loss of a sacramental

---

11. For the full treatment of these moments in history, see Trueman, *Strange New World*, 33–34 (Descartes), 34–42 (Rousseau), 52–59 (Marx), 59–68 (Nietzsche), 72–78 (Freud).

12. Taylor, *Secular Age*, 171–72.

ontology or what Taylor calls the immanentization of the world, individualism, and the particular moves which Trueman highlights with psychologized, politicized, and sexualized self. Overall, what I see happening when all things are combined and viewed together, is what I call *authority fatigue*. Society as a whole grew tired of authorities outside of themselves determining their way of life, their worldview, and ultimately their view of self and identity. The only answer to such a problem is to cut themselves off from such authorities, turn inward, and find that authority within themselves. Thus, what comes is what Taylor calls the "buffered self," as we discussed above. That is, all that enchanted world wherein all those transcendent forces could break in and where the "clerical elite" was necessary as something of guardians from those forces were wearing on the people. The people needed a world where they could just be themselves and be freed from the authority of the transcendent forces and the authority of the church that guarded them from it. Ultimately, this fatigue is what led to the shifts that Trueman outlines and what Kant called "enlightenment," which I outlined in the previous chapter.[13]

Now that I have connected recent discussions on EI, the history that I traced above, and what I will call authenticity throughout the rest of this chapter, it is time to move on to the discussion of that first model of identity. I will do this in two parts. First, I want to look at discussions around identity and disability and then identity and sexuality. My reason for approaching the discussion in this way is to avoid abstraction, root my look at identity models in particular examples, and show how an authenticity model of identity is ultimately about people being able to tell their own stories. Further, these two aspects of embodied particularities are often seen as antithetical to certain Christian understandings of identity, which will be a part of our exploration in the next chapter. Second, I will summarize my findings as well as give an appraisal of the model, taking into account the model's strengths and weaknesses, before wrapping up with a closing discussion on EI and the recent critiques of it in light of our look at the authenticity model.

AUTHENTICITY MODEL IN DISABILITY STUDIES

There are many issues to be aware of when seeking to engage in disability studies. Conversations abound on disability rights, proper terminology in

---

13. For a good history of this shift, particularly in younger generations in the mid-twentieth century, see Root, *Faith Formation in a Secular Age*.

speaking of persons with a disability, and, more recently, "disability identity." The latter two are both highly connected to conversations of identity and have much overlap.[14] For this reason, we will highlight recent explorations within disability studies to show particular expressions of an authenticity model of identity. This will allow us to avoid abstraction and show examples of how this works out in an individual's life.

Terminology within disability studies is a matter of categorization and, for many, speaks directly to another's identity. The categories in which we place people, or disabilities in general, say much about how we define and identify those persons. This is why many who write on the intersection of theology and disability choose to begin their work with a small conversation regarding terminology and the disability model with which they will proceed.[15] The first example of this can be seen in the concept of person-first language. Rather than saying "disabled people," we would choose to value the personhood first by saying "people with disabilities." To be conscious of this terminology is to be mindful of one's story and what part of this story is more valuable and vital as an identity marker: personhood.

However, Bethany McKinney Fox notes that while this may have, at one point, been the standard terminology, some pushed back, particularly deaf and autistic people. These particular communities felt that making such a point to refer to the aspect of disability second necessarily disparaged that aspect of their existence. Therefore, these persons chose to refer to and be referred to as deaf or autistic people, sometimes called identity-first language. "This demonstrates that there is no shame in being Deaf or autistic; rather, it is an aspect of their identity, enriching the diversity of humanity, and worth centering and celebrating."[16] It comes down to the story one wants to tell. For those in the deaf and autistic community, it would be inauthentic to remove this aspect of their history and denies an essential element of who they are.

We, as individuals, are not the only ones who get to tell our story, however. The culture around us often tells a larger story of which we are a part and thus affects how our narrative is understood, which is why many have still preferred the person-first language. The cultural story to which I am

---

14. Ultimately, the delineation is whether one is speaking of another person with a disability or those with a disability speaking of themselves, respectively.

15. For examples of this, see Fox, *Disability and the Way of Jesus*; Reynolds, *Vulnerable Communion*; Shurley, *Pastoral Care and Intellectual Disability*.

16. Fox, *Disability and the Way of Jesus*, 3.

referring here is a larger conversation within disability studies concerning the meta-narrative of disabilities in general and commonly discussed under the heading of disability models. Disability models offer different ways by which we are to think of disabilities and their relation to the humanity of a person and society more broadly. The most common understanding of disability is the "medical model," which locates disability as a sickness or illness due to physical and/or intellectual incapacities. The model comes from an understanding of what the norms of physical and intellectual wellness are and should look like; thus, a physical or intellectual dissent from that norm is considered a disability and thus outcasting the dissenters.

A cultural story of norms creates disagreement among the disability community on how they would like to be identified. Those who have been deeply ostracized seek to be identified as persons first as to be included in the community of humanity. However, others wish to change the cultural script so that this terminology debate is unnecessary. There are two primary ways of doing this. The first has been to think of disability in a different structure: "the social model." The social model sees disability as socially constructed in many cases. For instance, a person in a wheelchair is only *dis*abled because things or places are inaccessible due to a lack of ramp access and elevators. This thought has been influential in the disability rights movement and ultimately is what led to the Americans with Disabilities Act (ADA), which was passed by Congress in 1990 and later amended in 2008. This change in the model of disability allows those persons to authentically tell their story/express their identity without being misinterpreted as less than human because of their inability to live up to anthropological norms. Many of those within this marginalized community will no longer be genuinely understood as disabled because, through the change in societal understandings of the norm and access, they are able-bodied. This societally focused understanding of disability highlights a critical aspect of the authenticity model: Who gets to make personal identity claims? In the medical model, identity claims are made about a person with a disability. However, the social model paves a path for change in which the person with a disability might take back a part of themselves and live out their story more authentically.

The other way the cultural script can be combatted is found more within an individualistic framework than the more societally focused framework of the "social model" above. Partly in response to the social model, the "disability identity" approach seeks to claim disability as a positive identity, regardless of any social stigma or cultural script. Deborah Creamer, an American theologian with a disability, claims that her disability "is an essential part of who I am."[17] We also find such strong identity claims elsewhere. Cyndi Jones, the editor of *Mainstream Magazine*, is a polio survivor and was once asked if she would not "eagerly swallow a magic pill that would wipe away the lingering paralysis of her polio and let her walk again?"[18] Jones's answer is not what one might expect and is highly pointed, claiming no:

> It's the same thing as asking a black person would he change the color of his skin. . . . The main thing disabled people need to do is claim their disability and feel okay about it. Even if you don't like the way society treats you as a disabled person, it's part of your experience, it's part of how you come to be who you are.[19]

Therefore, one is emancipated from the bonds of marginalization and social stigma not by changing the social circumstances that have interpreted those persons as disabled but by an individual act of self-affirmation that "defies the symbolic meaning of one's disability of what should not be."[20] This self-affirmation and representation take a name used to demean and defame and use it as a positive term of self-respect and dignity.[21]

In the end, for a large cohort of the disability community, one's true identity is not found in the social surroundings that interpret or construe their history, nor is it found just in those historical events or facts of a person's life. Instead, it is located in the individual's authentic representation of themselves. Said differently, it is in their *telling* of their history. Though this authenticity model can most clearly be seen in the "disability identity" group I outlined last, it can also be seen in the social model. Even in the social model, they still seek for society to allow them to tell their story authentically. That is, traditions of the norm disable them via lack of access to living authentically whole lives. The social model and disability rights movement seek to deconstruct these traditions and open up ways of living

---

17. Creamer, "Finding God in Our Bodies," 73.
18. Shapiro, *No Pity*, 14.
19. Shapiro, *No Pity*, 14.
20. Reinders, *Receiving the Gift of Friendship*, 65.
21. Reinders, *Receiving the Gift of Friendship*, 65. Note that many constructionist accounts of disability reject such notions of "disability identity" in order to avoid essentialist claims. Recognizing these statements as one of identity2 rather than an ontological/identity1 statement is important, thus avoiding such critiques.

and representing themselves more authentically so that their identity can be expressed and known.

Furthermore, a difference between the medical model and the social and disability identity models is the allowance for individualism in one's story of disability. In the medical model, disabilities become larger categories or pools to which large groups of people can be linked as a statistic. There is little to no room for the expressive individualism of a disabled person in the medical model. That part of their story ends with the description that they are deaf or paralyzed. Even in what is known as an autism spectrum, the medical model tends to hold on to two categories of either high or low-functioning autism, which completely eradicates a spectrum and is, in fact, entirely misleading and damaging to the actual experiences of autistic people. Therefore, no one can truly express their own individual experiences in a medical model that seeks to category-dump people into their respective medical camps. Therefore, the social and disability-identity models allow for more individual expression for each disabled person.

AUTHENTICITY MODEL IN STUDIES OF SEXUALITY AND GENDER

As I did above, in highlighting identity construction through the literature of disability studies, I will seek here to show another instance of the authenticity model. In this section, I will draw attention to the language of identity construction within recent literature on gender and sexuality.

Few issues are more contentious within public discourse than that of sexuality and gender. Much of the reason for this is that, no matter the side of the discussion, the statements being made are understood by those in the LGBTQ+ community as statements of identity. This can be seen in the announcement made by Facebook in 2014, after they launched over fifty gender options to choose from, stating, "We want you to feel comfortable being your true, authentic self. An important part of this is the expression of gender, especially when it extends beyond the definitions of just 'male' or 'female.' So today, we're proud to offer a new custom gender option to help you better express your own identity on Facebook."[22]

For those in the LGBTQ+ community, the enlightenment and postmodern shift has been their liberator.[23] This is because feelings of same-sex

---

22. Quoted in Rosner, *Known by God*, 49.
23. The following paragraphs are indebted to Nancy Pearcey's discussion of this topic

attraction (SSA) and gender dysphoria have been broadly understood as personal feelings which go against biological, genetic, physiological, and chromosomal facts. In that instance, where does one find and base their identity? Feelings are true and cannot be neglected or trivialized, but do those facts take precedence over those of biology or other "hard" sciences? In a Kantian world, the answer is a resounding "Yes and amen!" Of Kant's influence on the world and understanding of the self, Robert Solomon writes that "the self becomes not just the focus of attention but the entire subject-matter of philosophy. . . . The self is not just another entity in the world, but in an important sense it creates the world."[24]

It is important to note that I do not wish to say that all within the LGBTQ+ community hold to a postmodern ethic, but it is this ethic that has created the cultural milieu that makes these new sexual ethics not just acceptable but seemingly natural. This is seen clearly when Camille Paglia wrote, "We have absolute claim to our bodies and may do with them as we see fit."[25] Nancy Pearcey reveals the authenticity understanding of identity within studies of gender and sexuality when she states that "Secular culture presents a 'gay script' that many find very compelling. It is a script that says anyone who experiences same-sex desires has discovered their authentic self, and that they will be most fulfilled by openly affirming it as their true identity."[26]

This narrative or script language can also be seen in a 2012 revision of a book titled *Gay Identity, New Storytelling and the Media* by Christopher Pullen, the senior lecturer in media theory at Bournemouth University. In the preface, he states that the book "offers a critical introduction to gay and lesbian identity within the media, focusing on the potential of 'new storytelling', foregrounding the potential of self-narrative, as fluid and enabling. . . . In exploring the potential of self-reflexive storytelling, gay men and lesbians challenge identity concerns, and offer new expressions of liberty." He continues, "[This book] is not an exposure of different experience; rather it is a celebration of diverse yet confluent mobilised narratives."[27] We see

---

in the chapter entitled "Body Impolitic" in her book *Love Thy Body*, 155–92.

24. Solomon, *Continental Philosophy since 1750*, 6.

25. Paglia, *Vamps and Tramps*, 71.

26. Pearcey, *Love Thy Body*, 166. I want to note that, while I do not entirely like the language Pearcey uses here, nor do I agree with her approach everywhere in her work, I do find the term "script" to be relevant in light of a narrative identity.

27. Pullen, *Gay Identity, New Storytelling*, xiii–xiv.

THE AUTHENTICITY MODEL

here something of validity to what Pearcey noted earlier. While discussion around either the importance or perceived dangers of LGBTQ+ representation in media from a Christian perspective is one that we cannot fully engage in this work, however, I think it important to note that Pullen does see gay identity narratives in different forms of media to be a place in which the LGBTQ+ community can engage and find something of their own story and find "new expressions of liberty." To put it another way, they can take a cue for their own liberating script of individual expression from the script of the media portrayal of authentic LGBTQ+ characters.

In an insightful volume, Bronwyn Fielder and Douglas Ezzy interview several LGBTQ+ Christians who are a part of the Australian Metropolitan Community Church (MCC) and the Uniting Church. Throughout, they weave stories from this sample of LGBT MCC and Uniting Church members. In their chapter titled "Seeking an Authentic Self," they share the stories of two transgender women whom they call Nova and Sylvie, who seek "the grace to be myself" (Nova) and to be "who I am" (Sylvie). All of this is a part of living into their identity and being true to themselves.[28] Sylvie even seeks to "underpin" everything by her spirituality and therefore "questions what would make God happy and concludes that the right to do is to transition to 'be who I am.'" The authors continue, "Both Nova and Sylvia illustrate the dialogical nature of self-identity: as they search for the 'true self', they seek answers through a dialogue with God."[29] It is important to note the ways that the interviewees and authors tie their "expressive individualism" to living out not just an authentic life and identity, but an authentic faith and spirituality as well. This is a perfect example of, as we noted earlier, the intersection of expressive individualism, authenticity, and identity. The interviewees' "feelings" or individual inner psychology[30] must be expressed outwardly even to recognize one's own identity and to be fully known by others. To not let these inner feelings dictate outward expression is to lie to oneself and to others, shown by the language of "true self" and "seeking the truth" about oneself.

It is clear that important conversations are happening on sexual identity within the church. Contrary to those above, some identify as LGBTQ+ and affirm a traditional, or as some may consider it, a "conservative" Christian sexual ethic, thus living either in celibacy or in what is often called a

---

28. Throughout, the authors quote and rely on the language of Taylor, *Ethics of Authenticity*.
29. Fielder and Ezzy, *Lesbian, Gay, Bisexual and Transgender Christians*, 60–61.
30. Trueman, *Rise and Triumph*, 23.

"mixed-orientation" marriage.³¹ The conversation among these Christians is to what extent, if at all, they should see their gender or sexuality as a defining factor in their identity. I want to note here that the following section surveys those who have argued that their sexuality is, in a real way, an aspect of their identity. In addition, they would all argue that their identity is grounded in their union with Christ as well. However, they have had to argue against a view that would essentially advocate an erasure of their sexuality in light of their conversion and regeneration because it is ultimately a fallen sexuality. For this reason, and others that will become evident later, I have decided to include them in this chapter on this authenticity model. Their sexuality, they would argue, is an authentic part of who they are, and that to express this in some way (e.g., calling themselves a "gay Christian") is part of what it means to even live authentically into their identity, even if that is primarily found "in Christ."

In Gregory Coles's personal memoir, he recounts a conversation with his pastor in which he was asked what his response would be to criticisms of claiming a gay identity when he should allow his identity as a Christian to eclipse those matters of sexual identity. While Coles is explicit that he would not want his sexual identity to alter his identity as a Christian, he does believe that it is important to recognize the diversity within Christianity: "Identity labels don't change who we are in Christ, but they do give us important information about how our *journeys of faith* might look different."³² Note Coles's language of "journeys" and how it maps to the authenticity model we have been discussing in terms of a story or narrative. Though he may not use the language of authenticity, he is speaking of the differences in the individual stories of Christians and the importance of not eclipsing these narratives with our religious identity. This is in line with a statement that he makes earlier in the book that his sexuality is "central to my identity."³³ His conversation with his pastor continues, "historically, when we've ignored differences in identity, people in the majority have tended to ignore the unique needs and challenges of minority identities. . . . sometimes we wind up only caring for the people who are easier to care for, the white people and rich people and able-bodied people. I think there's

---

31. For stories of those who identify as SSA living in celibacy see, Bennett, *War of Loves*; Coles, *Single, Gay, Christian*; Hill, *Washed and Waiting*. For stories of those living in "mixed-orientation" marriages, see Collins, *All But Invisible*; Gilson, *Born Again This Way*; Krieg and Krieg, *Impossible Marriage*; Perry, *Gay Girl, Good God*.

32. Coles, *Single, Gay, Christian*, 69 (italics added).

33. Coles, *Single, Gay, Christian*, 37.

value in naming both the majorities and the minorities, so we can remind ourselves who we might be forgetting."[34] Coles homes in, from a pastoral perspective, on the sort of erasure that other identity models can result in for those who would lay claim to diverse characterizations of identity. The full expression of the individual self is necessary to be fully known.

In a more philosophically and theologically oriented discussion on this intersection of sexuality and identity, Nate Collins focuses on the philosophy of aesthetics in his book *All But Invisible*. Collins seeks to reorient the reader to an understanding of attraction towards beauty, which is intrinsic to all human persons. This is contrary to the idea of exclusively sexual orientation and identity, which he argues is a rather new idea entrenched firmly in Western culture.[35] For this reason, he prefers not to use "the term sexual identity except in contexts in which the subject matter is explicitly sexual in nature."[36] This intrinsic desire for beauty is what he calls "aesthetic orientation"; he concludes that if it "is a deeply human experience, then it seems hard to avoid the conclusion that my aesthetic orientation can fundamentally influence the ways I experience my personhood."[37] The influence can be one of diminution or enhancement depending on the response; however, it can be seen from this discussion that to deny it entirely is to be inauthentic to one's self.[38] If we look at Collins's discussion in terms of Peterson's "created" and "constructed" identities, perhaps it is best to say that the danger, for Collins, lies in whether one would discuss their sexual identity in terms of being a created identity in a way that would determine it as a *creational* good. Though, it is hard to see how simply claiming certain sexuality as a matter of identity in terms of characterization naturally entails or even implies creational good.[39]

---

34. Coles, *Single, Gay, Christian*, 69.

35. Collins, *All But Invisible*, 131–49.

36. I will continue to use the language of sexual identity for what I think is its clarity and ubiquity in the literature on this topic.

37. Collins, *All But Invisible*, 151.

38. Near the end of the book, he notes that it is on these points of intersection of faith, sexuality, and identity that he disagrees with Rosaria Butterfield and others who would argue that "the gay identity belongs exclusively within the realm of the flesh." See Collins, *All But Invisible*, 300n7.

39. It is important to recognize the difference between something being a creational good and someone being born a certain way. One does not necessarily entail the other, such that denying a particular identity as a creational good does not mean one cannot be born that way.

PART 2 | MODELS OF IDENTITY

In the discussion of identity within sexuality and gender studies, we see the authenticity model in full bloom. One cannot discover their true identity even within their body's own natural way of presenting it. Rather, one's identity can only be known through their own interpretation of their body and their authentic sexual expression.[40]

It seems evident that there is a strong cultural script that values one's own interpretation and feeling of themselves over what their body tells them. This script within gender and sexuality studies is fascinatingly continuous and discontinuous with the feelings of those within the disability community. Their belief in authenticity as the true path to discovering one's identity is the same. However, for those persons with a disability, their bodies cannot be ignored or disregarded as a superfluous, physiological fact. They must listen to, accept, and embrace their bodies. Therefore, for one, the body might be the most authentic and individual expression of the self. For another, such as Nova and Sylvie, the body might be at odds with what is most true about a person, and they must therefore fight against their body in order to express their "true" identity.

As was also seen, there is a constituent of the Christian community that views their sexuality and gender or their disability as fundamental to their identity and is, therefore, to be necessarily and authentically expressed, though this expression may be done in different ways. Finally, it is important to note that there are many other ways that one might authentically represent their identity. This authenticity understanding might be seen in terms of race, ethnicity, culture, or education. Indeed, for many, true authenticity would be an expression of each of these categories together as that which makes them their particular and individual self. Yet, there is a wider understanding of identity within the church that has responded to this view of authenticity or self-representation, which we look at in the next chapter.

APPRAISAL OF THE AUTHENTICITY MODEL

Before exploring and engaging with the "in-Christ" model, I want to note what I think are some of the particular problems with the authenticity

---

40. It is important to note that "authentic sexual expression" does not require one identifying as LGBTQ+ to engage in sexual intimacy. Either celibacy or mixed-orientation marriage is, for the Christian who holds to a traditional Christian sexual ethic, an authentic expression of their sexuality as they are the only possible expression of their sexuality according to this ethic.

model. This model of identity has a massive following for the majority of the culture. As was mentioned above, such an understanding is a result of the secular age. Expressive individualism is a large means by which we buffer ourselves from the cross-pressures of transcendent and immanent worldviews. One example of such "buffering," according to Alan Noble, is in the ways in which we make the weightier things of life, such as beliefs in the transcendent or other beliefs with rich explanatory power, more about identity signaling. In other words, matters worthy of deep contemplation and thorough understanding are relegated to "thin beliefs."[41] These matters simply *represent* who we are rather than *transform* who we are. Such a distinction is important as authenticity, in a post-modern age, commonly chooses to represent one's self (and the beliefs that express that identity) by signaling "thin" beliefs based on *a priori* assumptions. This is in contrast to allowing time and contemplation on serious matters that concern and affect ourselves and others to transform us as individuals and our beliefs as they change or grow through their strengthening from other voices and influences. The latter, however, is not often seen as authentic due to its being influenced by culture and the voices of others.

We are now faced with two important questions regarding the fixity and malleability of identity. To what degree is one's identity made up of those changing factors, and to what degree is it marked by the fixed aspects of one's life? A true "authentic" identity must necessarily be founded on both factors; it needs room to change as we change while requiring a stable ground to secure us from any external transcendent force. That stability within the "authenticity model" seems to be found in the supreme autonomy of humanism: a focus on the self. Herein lies a problem that is raised by the primary question of Vernon White in his volume *Identity*.[42] The rapid pace of change within our society raises the question regarding the security and confidence one might find in the stability of one's self. It seems that the new transcendent—one for which we have no buffer—is the rapidly changing society that forces us to change with it. Thus, it seems that two competing mantras plague the authenticity model: "Change with the times *or* you'll get left behind" and "Change with the times *and* you'll get left behind."[43] That is, in one way, an *authentic* identity must naturally

---

41. Noble, *Disruptive Witness*, 44–45.

42. White, *Identity*.

43. My thinking of these as mantras is influenced by my listening to the song "Conversation with the Sky" by Abandon Kansas.

change with society and culture in order to be authentic to the self which is inevitably changed by that society. However, on the other hand, to change with the rapidly shifting culture around us is to lose one's authentic self as merely a product of your environment, maintaining no autonomous control and eroding the once-held confidence in our ability to create our own destiny and identity.[44]

Therefore, while the authenticity model has embedded within a great strength of seeking identity (which assumes some degree of stability) within inevitable change, it seeks it in a place that it cannot be found: the inherently unstable, individual self, which, as we saw, is truly a product of the surrounding culture. That is, identity is a search and rightful desire for stability of the self, but identity in the second sense is something that cannot stay entirely static either, as it is inevitably informed by the change that one experiences in life. Thus, the stable structure going by the name of identity is attempted by some to be built in the name of authenticity, which is a foundation of rapid movement and change. It seems the authenticity model is like the foolish man who built his house on the sand: within this model, our identity is eventually shaken and torn down by the fickle winds of societal change. Or, in some cases, it is shaken and torn down by our choice of drastic change. Recall the stories of Nova and Sylvie earlier in which they described their journey of authenticity and identity as "really re-structuring myself" (Nova) and "tearing her life apart and rebuilding it" (Sylvie).[45]

Such major and rapid changes, which, in some cases, are even destructive/reconstructive, run into what is often called the persistence problem. We will avoid getting tangled up in the weeds of such philosophical debates; however, the question of the persistence of identity in terms of characterization, or what I have called personal identity, is an important one in terms of authenticity. Put another way, it may be argued that a drastic, voluntary change must be made in one's expression of identity to more faithfully live into their authentic self, making their identity expression prior to their change something of a lie or false self. However, the question must then be raised: What makes this self truly authentic in light of future change (voluntary or otherwise) that may occur? This is the problem of authenticity, the issue of stability or persistence through time and change.

---

44. White, *Identity*, 3.
45. Fielder and Ezzy, *Lesbian, Gay, Bisexual and Transgender Christians*, 60.

THE AUTHENTICITY MODEL

This issue is why others, particularly those who characterize and define identity as being found "in Christ," will argue that the authenticity approach to identity is too great of a focus on identity in the second sense. That is, those holding to "authenticity" have wrongly focused on who they are defined by means of the world around them and too little on who they were truly made to be. Said differently, it is too great a focus on "constructed" identities over "created" identities. Whoever we are today is a post-Genesis 3, constructed version of who we are supposed to be, and defining ourselves too deeply based on this version of ourselves is to ignore certain implications of the redemption of Christ. We must, therefore, find our identity in the redemption that Christ offers us. An example of this can be seen in response to those who make sexual identity claims alongside claims of Christian identity.

In Denny Burk and Heath Lambert's book *Transforming Homosexuality*, they respond to the identity statement of being a "gay Christian," saying that "to embrace an identity that goes against God's revealed purpose is by definition sinful."[46] That is, when broadened out, to embrace ourselves as we are is sinful because, in this world, we inherently live against God's revealed purpose. Elsewhere, they clarify, "we are who God says we are." We are not who our sinful desires say that we are.[47] This critique gets at the truth that our understanding of ourselves, and thus the starting point for our identity, is often not in line with objective reality as God created it. While I understand and agree with the basic sentiment of this statement, I do not think, as I will explore more deeply in the next chapter, that their statement considers the nuances of how sinful desires play a part in our narrative, which forms our identity. The words of David Bennett are helpful here, "When Christians receive Christ, we repent of what is sinful. But we don't renounce our individual humanity, which is shaped both by God and by our experience in this fallen world and this fallen body." Later he compares this to the reformative nature of Paul's identity and his being a Jew: "Paul was a Jew. That identity he was born with was an integral part of his life and his relationship with Messiah Jesus. However, his view of Judaism and how he related to it changed."[48] Further, we will see later how Burk and Lambert do not even maintain consistency in their understanding regarding the effect that sinful desires have on our identity. With this, I

---

46. Burk and Lambert, *Transforming Homosexuality*, 37.
47. Burk and Lambert, *Transforming Homosexuality*, 36.
48. Bennett, *War of Loves*, 213, 215.

will now look at this model of identity: What does it mean for one's identity to be "in Christ"?

EXPRESSIVE INDIVIDUALISM REVISITED

In light of our look at the authenticity model from the perspective of Christian and non-Christian thinkers, I think it is important to revisit EI for just a moment and think through the concerns before entering into a discussion on the "in Christ" model in the next chapter. A general concern of EI and one that I myself hold and discuss at length in chapter 2 is the concern of the individualism piece. It is a truism in theological anthropology that a fundamental aspect of personal identity is the necessary social component. That is, we were created as social beings, made to be in relation with others. Often, and rightly so, this is confirmed on the basis of the creation narrative in Gen 1 and 2 and the divinely declared quality of "not good" for man to be alone.[49] Thus, any ideology that prizes an individualistic outlook on identity strikes as antithetical to Scripture and "not good." However, EI, at a close look, is clearly not as solely individualistic as the name might suggest. In fact, EI necessitates a social reception of one's individualistic expression. Therefore, EI may even be less individualistic than some critics may think. In addition, as I will show in the next chapter, some of the concerns within evangelical theology around the "expressive" part of EI as a negative value can be misplaced or overstated.

That being the case, this does not necessarily let EI off the hook entirely. There are healthier and more problematic versions of any school of thought. The healthier forms are not to be feared and ought to be engaged for what they might teach us. For those problematic forms, some of which we saw above, I think the recognition that EI is less individualistic than some of its proponents suggest or think it is—and certainly, less than its philosophical predecessors, such as Enlightenment thinking, suggest—lends itself toward a different, though not unrelated, critique. Such an expressive form of individualism, which naturally requires a community to which one expresses oneself, raises the question of how authentic such an expression is. That is to say, the outside pressure from one's community to express themselves becomes an authority that strips the individual of the

---

49. Many confirm this on the basis of the nature of the triune God as a relational God and our being created in his image. For these arguments, see Harrison, *God's Many-Splendored Image*; Zizioulas, *Being as Communion*; Volf, *After Our Likeness*.

autonomy that they have sought through the inward turn. It will be good to bear all this in mind as we look toward the next model of identity and my proposal for a sacramental identity in part 3.

4

The "Identity in Christ" Model

ANOTHER CATEGORY BY WHICH many think through their identity is through the lens of religious identity. The dominant understanding within the church is that our identity, or at least our core identity, is to be found in our union or participation with Christ. Such thinking is often spoken of as seeing our identity "in Christ."

In this chapter, I will explore such a view of identity. There are two particular versions of this model that I will explore here. The first will be one that I see as promoting something of an erasure of personal narrative. In seeking to focus language of identity in our union with Christ, an admirable desire, it trades on ignoring the embodied and storied aspects of our individual humanity. We will look at this version through a couple of notable works written on identity, but also through the personal stories of some who have experienced this sort of erasure in pastoral conversations or church contexts.

The second version is one that I think seeks to faithfully balance both the realities of embodied identity and the new identity that we take on in our union with Christ. Two New Testament scholars have recently published works on personal identity from a biblical and theological perspective: Brian Rosner and Klyne Snodgrass. They have sought to shed light on our union with Christ as a stabilizing grounding for our identity in the midst of fast pace changes that impact our embodied lives and stories. Therefore, these examinations of our identity "in Christ" are careful to avoid the problems of erasure. However, as we will see later, I do not believe they satisfactorily answer the questions of identity raised by the authenticity model.

After exploring these different versions of the "in-Christ" model, I will offer a brief summary and appraisal as I did in the last chapter. This will draw part 2 to a close and allow us to move forward toward a new model of personal identity.

NARRATIVE ERASURE VERSIONS

As seen in the previous chapter, some Christian thinkers view their individual stories as what defines them, whether their disability, sexuality, gender, age, ethnicity, or otherwise. However, some Christians hold to a view of identity that would say our embodied narrative is eclipsed by our union with Christ. An example can be seen in the story of Richard Twiss, a Native American theologian. Twiss's pastor relayed this belief to him as he wrestled with the relationship between his newfound faith and his native heritage. Based on Gal 3:28, the pastor told Twiss, "So, Richard, don't worry about being Indian anymore—just be like us."[1] The pastor shows his understanding of the in-Christ model as one that implies erasure, or as Twiss would rightly and appropriately call it, colonization. Twiss uses the language of colonization here, throughout both of his books, because he sees this understanding of identity as a continuation of the colonization of First Nations people, and he also calls it "a kind of cultural genocide."[2] Throughout Twiss's book, he recounts the tension from being taught that participation with Christ brought a new identity that left the old one behind, "In reference to my Native culture, I was informed that the Bible said, 'Touch not the unclean thing,' or 'come out from among them and be separate,' or 'what fellowship does light have with darkness?' This meant I needed to leave my Indian ways behind me because I had a new identity in Christ and it *was not* Indian!"[3]

Earlier in the book, Twiss tells the story that indicates from where such an understanding of identity comes. In the story, a man whom Twiss had known for some time said to him, "Well Richard, don't you think it's better for your people that we, a Christian democracy, conquered your people?"[4] Several things are wrong with such a horrific statement, and Twiss responds to those issues in the pages that follow in his book. My concern

---

1. Twiss, *Rescuing the Gospel from the Cowboys*, 104.
2. Twiss, *One Church Many Tribes*, 28.
3. Twiss, *Rescuing the Gospel from the Cowboys*, 82 (emphasis original).
4. Twiss, *Rescuing the Gospel from the Cowboys*, 62.

is the ways in which this statement reflects a theological foundation for a version of this identity model that tends to erase the embodied realities of a person. What we see in this statement is something that Twiss notes at the beginning of the same chapter: cultural interpretation of Scripture. That is, we all interpret Scripture through our own cultural experience; it's impossible not to. The problems start when we assume that our reading, through our own particular experience, is the correct way to read.[5] It is this sort of understanding that leads to the erasure form of the "in Christ" model and statements like the one we saw above. When we believe we are reading and constructing a theology from a culturally blank slate, our theological models become rigid and leave no room for narrative, thus no room for things like what the subtitle of Twiss's book suggests: "A Native American expression of the Jesus way." Therefore, a cultural and theological assumption is at play when the man says what he did or Twiss's pastor says, "Don't worry about being Indian anymore—just be like us."[6] The erasure model comes out of an assumption that our way (i.e., any particular way) of reading and living out our union with Christ is the "biblical" way or the transcendent way, that is to say, the way God intended. Please don't misunderstand me, I am *not* saying that there is no Truth or that there is no "way it's supposed to be." To slip into such understanding would be to simply fall into a strong "authenticity" model in which we are to "live *our* truth." What I am talking about here is recognizing that all persons who live out their identity "in Christ" live out *storied* expressions of identity "in Christ."[7] I confess that to be "in Christ" also means to be under the rule and reign of *the* Christ, that is, the anointed King, and therefore requires submitting to his way of kingdom life. However, his kingdom is a diverse one filled with people who have rich stories.

We see another form of this erasure version in other places as well. Take for instance the response that Denny Burke and Heath Lambert gave above regarding sexual identity as a Christian. I quote them again here, "To embrace an identity that goes against God's revealed purpose is by

---

5. Twiss, *Rescuing the Gospel from the Cowboys*, 61. Citing McKnight, *Community Called Atonement*, 44.

6. Twiss, *Rescuing the Gospel from the Cowboys*, 104.

7. On a much smaller scale, this all seems akin to my traveling to Australia and assuming that I am accent-free because my way of pronouncing these words must be the right way, rather than simply being the way that is familiar to me, while failing to recognize that such thinking and ways of hearing are true for the Australian who hears me speak.

definition sinful."[8] Therefore, when we confess Christ and our union with him as our identity, then, to claim something else as our identity which goes against God's created order and purpose for one's life, we are in sin. This is why, for Burke and Lambert, identity claims such as those made by Bennett or Coles of being a "gay Christian" are by definition sinful and self-defeating, because they would argue that to be a Christian is to be transformed by Christ, to become a new person and to take on a new identity that puts sin to death, such as that of SSA. However, later we see Burke and Lambert failing to live up to their own criteria of identity language when they state, "Sin is not merely what we do. It is also *who we are*."[9] The incongruity lies in the fact that "who we are" is an identity statement that contradicts their statement that our identity must be found in the purposes revealed by God, as certainly our God-revealed purpose is not sinfulness. I have a hard time seeing what the difference is between recognizing our own embodied realities of sexual identity and stating them versus stating that our fundamental identity is our sinfulness. This is especially true since those who would make the identity claim of "gay Christian," such as Coles and Bennett, would argue that living into their sexual identity would be sinful. They are simply refusing to deny the embodied reality that their own romantic and sexual attraction is oriented toward persons of the same sex.

Such a rigid view of identity in Christ leaves one to wonder what a view might say to one who suffers a horrible trauma as a result of the forces of sin and death that inhabit our world, thus leaving the realities of one's embodied life forever changed. Would such a view require that person to not identify with such embodied realities because they go "against God's revealed purpose"? Views like this are not only theologically flawed but remain unhelpful for those in the midst of a genuine identity crisis. To tell someone who is searching for who they are and feels lost and confused in their search for their own self that their identity is "in Christ" now and that they need not worry about those other things may, in fact, only cause more trauma, as it essentially denies the realities of their story. We would do well to remember that what made it possible for us to be united with Christ was Jesus first coming into our own embodied realities and uniting himself with our own frail humanity. A theology of identity truly marked by the gospel must start with the good news of the incarnation.

---

8. Burk and Lambert, *Transforming Homosexuality*, 37.
9. Burk and Lambert, *Transforming Homosexuality*, 58 (emphasis added).

PART 2 | MODELS OF IDENTITY

PRIORITIZATION VERSIONS

Having discussed what I have called narrative erasure versions of the in-Christ model, I move on to what I believe is a much more faithful and pastorally sensitive version of the in-Christ identity. In fact, there is much to commend on the theological model of identity found in the authors that we will be discussing here, though they both fall short in some areas, as we will see in the last section of this chapter. I will call these "prioritization versions" because they see the matters of embodiment and personal narratives as important but derivatively so or as secondary to our primary identity, which is found in Christ.

Two NT scholars, Brian Rosner and Klyne Snodgrass, have written books on a biblical theology of personal identity in which they have a primary focus on who we are "in Christ," but without ignoring the embodied realities of one's life, which inevitably forms who they are as one united with Christ.[10] In fact, both authors dedicate chapters to the embodied realities of human life that inform our personal identity. We will look at both authors in turn, while noting some other scholars and their take on these matters along the way.

Brian Rosner has written two books on personal identity. The first, *Known by God*, is the more technical, biblical-theological work. His second, *How to Find Yourself*, is more focused on the cultural moment and the cultural interest in identity.[11] There is some content overlap between the two, and thus, we will talk about both here. In *Known by God*, Rosner argues that "being 'in Christ' is arguably the apostle Paul's most comprehensive answer to the question of personal identity."[12] Though within his work, Rosner does spend the entirety of chapter 3 working through eleven identity markers, such as age, ethnicity, sexuality, and the like, he concludes that Scripture teaches these to be "inadequate" foundations for identity. He makes this claim on the basis of reading Gal 3:28.[13] Rosner argues that this passage tells us that, in Christ, matters of ethnicity, social status, and gender are no longer of prime importance to one's identity.[14]

---

10. Rosner, *How to Find Yourself*; *Known by God*; Snodgrass, *Who God Says You Are*.
11. Rosner, *How to Find Yourself*, 17n3.
12. Rosner, *Known by God*, 140.
13. Rosner, *Known by God*, 63.
14. Grant Macaskill further claims from Gal 3:27–28 that, through one's union with Christ, "their identity is derivative of his," and J. Todd Billings asserts that our union with Christ is "our true identity, our real identity" (Macaskill, *Union with Christ in the New*

THE "IDENTITY IN CHRIST" MODEL

Rosner is careful, however, to make it clear that these "standard markers of identity remain essential for personal identity."[15] They simply don't tell the whole story.

It is difficult to see how Gal 3:28 or the similar Col 3:11 support such a view, though. The temptation is evident in what seems to be a clear contrast between our being "in Christ" and our ethnic or gendered embodied realities made by Paul. However, what Paul is referring to here is simply the relationship of these differences with their unity to God. Paul is claiming that Christ has torn down these walls of difference and that all are equally united to God in Christ, who is the very image of the invisible God (Col 1:15). Thus, these passages are a call not to lay down any individual identity, but to take up a new *collective* identity "in Christ." Not only does this collective identity "in Christ" not dissolve or undermine these embodied realities and differences, but it requires and celebrates them. Our collective identity "in Christ" is one of unity in diversity that can only be accomplished through Christ's reconciling work of the cross. Therefore, the evidence of diversity brings glory and honor to Christ and his unifying work.

Rosner ultimately frames his work around the proposal that being known by others, and ultimately God, "is critical to personal identity."[16] Rosner sees this understanding of identity as countercultural in light of the pervasive individualism of today's world because it finds one's identity "in connection with someone else."[17] He later frames the understanding in direct contention with the above model when he states that union with Christ does not negate the significance of our individual lives—"We do not lose our past stories. We remain individuals in the fullest sense"—however, "ultimately these events don't define us."[18] However, while it adds some nuance to the "in Christ" proposal, it is ultimately difficult to decipher how our identities remain narratively indexed in any significant way if the events of our story "don't define us," and thus, the statement seems a bit overstated. Despite this, I think he rightly argues that authenticity is a hazardous way of understanding the self, though it is the highest social currency. Rosner aptly points out that self-deception is a danger, and thus, authenticity is

---

Testament, 197; Billings, *Union with Christ*, 30).

15. Rosner, *Known by God*, 64.
16. Rosner, *Known by God*, 148.
17. Rosner, *Known by God*, 140.
18. Rosner, *Known by God*, 148.

rather difficult to sort out. Not to mention the narcissism to which the "true to yourself" narrative can lead.[19] In the end, identity must be found in relation to others, namely, the divine other, as we know God and are "known by God" via our union with Christ, his Son.

Another recent proposal for a Christian understanding of personal identity has been that of Klyne Snodgrass in *Who God Says You Are*. Though approaching the topic differently than Rosner, Snodgrass lands in the same broad camp. Snodgrass spends most of his project working through the traditional identity markers that might be found in an authenticity model through conversation on more general categories such as embodiment, individual history, relationships, etc. However, while it may sound like an articulation of self-representation as identity, these chapters outlining traditional identity markers are all prefaced by the opening proposal that faith transforms identity. Snodgrass states that the factors outlined in the book are true of all humans, "but all factors shaping our identity must be reconsidered from a Christian perspective."[20] He continues, "Faith, true faith, reframes identity. Faith means living out the identity God says you have, the identity given you *in Christ*."[21] I think this is something that Snodgrass gets right. His chapter on boundaries frames the relationship of "traditional identity markers" and "identity in Christ" well when he shows that "in Christ," these markers "must not be allowed to be the basis of denigration and exclusion. Christians must not erect boundaries that diminish and exclude people."[22] I agree with this view toward traditional identity markers. My contention with Snodgrass's model of identity comes more from his understanding of what identity is. Snodgrass seems to assume that to see ethnicity or other traditional identity markers as determinative for one's identity is to necessarily subordinate union with Christ or our identity as Christians.

It is evident that Snodgrass also offers something of an "in Christ" model of identity along with Rosner. The difference lies in the emphasis on what this means and looks like practically. His chosen approach through the narrative identity that is ultimately transformed allows a bit more for the language of authenticity, which is language to which Rosner is more averse. However, Snodgrass argues that genuine authenticity is living out

---

19. Rosner, *Known by God*, 234.
20. Snodgrass, *Who God Says You Are*, 32.
21. Snodgrass, *Who God Says You Are*, 34.
22. Snodgrass, *Who God Says You Are*, 188.

who we are *called* to be. But who are we called to be? The immediate answer to this question is ultimately found in those markers that Ryan Peterson has called "created identities," which Peterson ultimately boils down to our being created in the *imago Dei*.[23] Thus, given the fallenness of humanity, the New Testament's statements regarding Jesus as the full realization of the *imago Dei* in humanity and our redemption through our union with Christ, it is still "in Christ" by which one finds the "image of God" identity amidst a broken world. This is what Snodgrass is saying when he concludes:

> What we all need is authenticity of being, that we live in accord with our true selves, not just the self we think we want to be but the self God calls us to be. Knowing who we are is not something we acquire by ourselves. We know ourselves only by knowing our God. Knowing ourselves is less important than knowing who made us, calls us, goes with us, and *knows us*.[24]

Here, we see the similarity to Rosner's proposal in the language of knowing and being known. That is, our identity is found in traditional identity markers, but secondarily or derivatively so. Ultimately, our identity is found in knowing who we are in God and who he knows us to be, as the person he created and is making us to be in Christ. Such a claim is hard to disagree with or deny. And in fact, I don't wish to deny the basic claims made by Rosner or Snodgrass. What I find to be the problem with such a model is that it leaves one wanting because it does not speak to the identity questions that come up out of the embodied realities of life and, therefore, remains vague in the practicality of what such a model truly looks like in relationship with the traditional, embodied identity markers. In addition, the model leaves questions open regarding change and stability in one's identity through time.

Finally, I want to look at a recent work from Kevin P. Emmert, who has also proposed a view toward the sacraments for "Christian identity." Emmert's work is an important one as it draws in sacramental theology to discussions around one's identity in one's union with Christ. He opens with a statement that resonates with me deeply:

> In an age when countless people are struggling to understand their identity, Christians frequently tell one another, "Your identity is in Christ." This statement is often issued in attempts to

---

23. For more on this, see Peterson, "Created and Constructed"; and Peterson, *Imago Dei as Human Identity*.

24. Snodgrass, *Who God Says You Are*, 223 (emphasis original).

swiftly tranquilize anxiety when someone expresses uncertainty over place and purpose in life: Who am I? Do I belong? How do I find security? What is my purpose? Yet in many such cases, the adage does little to assuage unwelcome feelings of bewilderment. People often tout it without much elaboration, and thus it feels like a trope.[25]

I share this concern and frustration. However, I am concerned that Emmert's work does not offer elaboration on this truth in order to speak to the anxiety mentioned in the way that he thinks it does. Later, Emmert states, "We can rightly understand *who we are* only in relation to *who he is*. Personal identity is therefore not something we must discover on our own through our own narratives and pursuits but is something already granted to us in the Lord Jesus Christ. Simply put, our identity is not a construct to self-fabricate but a gift to receive."[26]

Emmert rightly wants to place high importance on the narrative of Christ and Scripture for the identity of Christians; however, due to a lack of careful language, he has seemingly negated the importance of the individual narratives that we bring with us as we enter into the story of God and the church. The above statement is not a full erasure of the sort spoken about above, but it pushes our embodied particularities to the side. This, in my experience of ministry in Portland, Oregon, serves as the basis of a person's anxiety around identity. How do they square the concrete realities of their embodied existence and the impact these realities have on their own understanding of their personal identity and this new Christian reality in which their identity is "in Christ"? Emmert states at the end of his introduction that this is not a question that he seeks to answer, "It is imperative that I mention at the outset that I do not intend to address the unique aspects of people's individuality—that is, what makes them persons distinct from others. Features of a person's particularity—from genetic makeup, personality, and family narrative to vocation, education, and hobbies, to name just a few—are not in view in this work."[27] That being said, it would

---

25. Emmert, *Water and the Blood*, 1.

26. Emmert, *Water and the Blood*, 3.

27. Emmert, *Water and the Blood*, 9–10. First, note how this highlights the importance of clarity around language. Up to this point, he has used the language of personal identity, which I have used throughout to speak of that identity in the second sense of self-conceptions and embodied particularities, etc., which he explicitly does not mean here.

Second, I fear that while Emmert does not address these matters throughout the rest

THE "IDENTITY IN CHRIST" MODEL

be unfair to level too much of a critique on Emmert for not accomplishing something that he did not set out to do. However, it is no less concerning that any attempt at constructing a truly theological understanding of personal identity could be made without considering and discussing the realities of our embodied existence and what this changes about the ways in which we can understand our identity in Christ.

Rosner and Snodgrass powerfully articulate recent developments in understanding identity in our union with Christ. Their arguments are thoroughly biblical, especially in their working through Paul's various usage of "εν χριστω" and other similar prepositional phrases. Along with the language of putting on the "new man" (Eph 4:24; Col 3:10) and putting off the "old man" (Rom 6:6; Eph 4:22; Col 3:9), Rosner and Snodgrass find much within the Pauline corpus to support their understanding that one's true identity is found not in those individual aspects of one's story; instead they are now found in Christ. As Rosner and Snodgrass, along with other proponents of the in-Christ model, note, it is not that these aspects of an individual's life are no longer essential or of no value but they are transformed and no longer define us.

We see a similar interpretation in G. K. Beale's commentary on Colossians, "Of course, Christians still retain an ethnic identity, but their ultimate identity is in Christ, the true Israel and new Adam, where such distinctions do not finally define who a person is."[28] While he may be referring to our "final" eschatological identity, it is difficult to see how this assuages the problem of his interpretation of an identity "in Christ." He further elaborates by pointing to the connection between this verse and that in Gal 3, saying, "In the new creation there are no nationalistic or racial distinctions that determine a person's ultimate identity. The only determiner of that identity in that new sphere is 'Christ.'"[29] Many other contemporary commentators, while not as forthright in identity claims from these passages,

---

of the work, he has already addressed them enough in the statements prior to signaling how he understands their importance in a theological construction of identity. These two comments combined could send the wrong message that these embodied particularities take a backseat in a truly theological understanding of personal identity.

28. Beale, *Colossians and Philemon*, 285.

29. Beale, *Colossians and Philemon*, 286. Though here he is speaking of the "new creation" it should be understood that it seems that Beale is not speaking only of the fully renewed creation that comes with the fully consummated kingdom of God, but rather the new creation that we experience now, which is inaugurated in Christ and points toward that greater reality to come.

make similar arguments as Beale does: not that Paul has any desire to eradicate all gender, ethnic, or socio-economic distinctions entirely but rather he seeks to show how our union with Christ becomes the ultimate grounding for our identity. Thus, these embodied distinctions, though they remain, do not make final claims on our identity upon our union with Christ.[30]

However, this way of understanding our old identity markers is only helpful as further elaboration is given to how one might rightly think through their identity on these new terms. Without this guidance, we see this model lead to problematic frameworks such as colorblind ideologies and even the dismissal of gender binaries.[31] That is, if our identities are not connected to our embodied experiences, but only "in Christ" in ways that do not even center Christ's embodied life, then a space is opened for questioning the importance of these distinctions any longer.[32] In the end, both of these views ultimately must face up to the difficulty of the embodied particularities of the resurrected Christ. Jesus' resurrection body remains indexed by distinctions of sex and ethnicity. His body even gains a new physical marker of the scars on his hands, feet, and side.

APPRAISAL OF THE IN-CHRIST MODEL

As can be seen in the critique against authenticity, this model of identity takes into account that we are a people in formation still, and thus, to base

---

30. For contemporary commentators with this view, see Dunn, *Epistles to the Colossians and to Philemon*, 223–27; Moo, *Letters to the Colossians and to Philemon*, 270–73; Osborne, *Colossians and Philemon*, 101–4; Thompson, *Colossians and Philemon*, 77–80. Furthermore, it should be added there are some ancient interpreters who saw Gal 3:28 in particular as revealing that gender distinctions would themselves disappear in the new creation and thus as the ideal for humanity. Gregory of Nyssa is particularly known for this interpretation in *On the Making of Man*. For modern investigations of Gregory's view, see Boersma, *Embodiment and Virtue in Gregory of Nyssa*; Coakley, "Eschatological Body," 61–73; and *God, Sexuality, and the Self*; Harrison, "Gender, Generation, and Virginity in Cappadocian Theology," 38–68.

31. For proponents of this latter interpretation, see DeFranza, *Sex Difference in Christian Theology*; Hartke, *Transforming*; Meeks, "Image of the Androgyne," 165–208.

32. It is important to note here the difference between interpreting these and similar passages as arguing for an eradication of these embodied distinctions and the eradication of meaning in these embodied distinctions. While it is impossible to truly understand these passages as arguing that the ontological differences are eliminated altogether, an "in-Christ" model, as we have been exploring, easily lends itself toward an explanation that the deeper anthropological meaning or purpose behind these differences are null and void for identity purposes.

THE "IDENTITY IN CHRIST" MODEL

our identity entirely on ourselves as we are and not who we are on the road to being is inherently flawed. Seeking our identity in Christ means that we are seeking to find our identity in the redeemed life offered to us in and through Christ's living example of human life and work on the cross. In other words, the "in-Christ" model does seek to respond to the issue that we saw in the authenticity model, where it seems to fail to see the stability of identity in the language itself. Yet, with its proposed answer to the problem, the "in-Christ" model seems to find itself in a different but related problem in which it zeroes in too narrowly on the stable nature of identity and fails to take into proper consideration or focus the changing nature of one's identity. Again, to be fair to the works of Rosner and Snodgrass, they recognize this changing nature of identity. However, the focus is always on how one's identity is in the stabilizing truth of one's union with Christ. I concede to this fact, it is a scriptural truth and a hopeful one, but one that fails to speak to these particular questions of identity when not paired properly with the unstable and ever-changing realities of embodied life that bear on our identity.

It might be argued that speaking to such a deficiency is easy enough. We might simply look to the created/constructed binary of Peterson or take a note from Burk and Lambert regarding finding our identity in God's created purposes. We are still *living into* (change) our created purposes or created identities (stability), but such a change takes place only in the context of our union with Christ. Once again, I can agree with the basic premise of the statement, but a question of the typical language used here is that it is difficult to see how this can be differentiated from spiritual formation and sanctification.[33]

So, the question remains: What does it look like, practically speaking, to find one's self in Christ? Could one say that our *new* authentic self is simply found by an inward turn where one finds salvation and union with Christ? It is difficult to see where Scripture supports such inward and isolated views of one's union with Christ and integration into God's kingdom people. Indeed, we are no longer a slave to sin; we are renewed in

---

33. I am grateful to Patrick Schreiner, who served as the director of the ThM program at Western Seminary when I was defending my thesis. He asked essentially this question regarding the differentiation between spiritual formation and identity. The question has plagued me since. This question, I think, comes out of the way Christian models of identity tend to fail in their focus on traditional identity markers by lapsing into more ethereal and disembodied ways of speaking about identity. Now, while I do believe there is some overlap between the two, I hope to show where the differences lie in part 3.

and by Christ. However, we still await the full consummation of what the work of Christ has done. We are still in the stages of this redemptive drama in which we must "practice resurrection."[34] The new person that we are in Christ is still being nurtured and growing and, therefore, cannot yet be fully known to ourselves, and we should expect that our practice within the drama is done on a stage with a host of others. Again, I am not saying that the understanding of finding one's identity in Christ is wrong; it is, however, incomplete and oftentimes unguided. The answer to the question of identity gives us the right set of questions with which to begin. Our identity is something we have, express, and are living in as much as it is something that we are living into as it changes with our stories. How do we bring our changing, embodied selves to Christ and find peace and stability in the present turbulence of our stories? In the final two chapters, I will argue that the answer to this question is ultimately found in one's participation in the sacraments of the church. Such a view combats the rampant expressive individualism of the authenticity model with an ecclesial model that also offers a solution to the problems of change and stability found in authenticity. However, as I will show, a sacramental model is also firmly rooted in the scriptural claims of being in Christ while grounding our union with Christ in storied and embodied realities and a more incarnational and embodied Christology.

---

34. See Peterson, *Practice Resurrection*; and Vanhoozer, *Faith Speaking Understanding*, for this language of "redemptive drama" and "practice resurrection."

PART 3

A Sacramental Identity

IN PART 3, I will offer a constructive account of personal identity, its formation, and its stabilization through time and the changes that occur. Despite the narratively indexed nature of a person's identity, the sacraments stabilize or fix our identity in the redemptive narrative of Christ and his kingdom. I will examine the sacraments of baptism, the Eucharist, and confession[1].

I will begin in chapter 5 by looking at history to see what three past authors and theologians have written about these sacraments and how they shape a person's identity. The purpose of the chapter will be two-fold. First, we all stand on the shoulders of giants, and as a theologian, I seek to do my work in the communion of the saints and the tradition of the church catholic. Such a task involves taking my cue from those who have come before on what has been confessed regarding the sacraments and what it means to be human. Second, placing my constructive account in the tradition of such thinkers will firm up my interpretation that the modern models of identity—the authenticity model and the formulations of the "in-Christ" model—which we looked at in part 2 are just that, models of *modernity* and products of the "secular age" in which we now live.

The final chapter (chapter 6) will explain why I have chosen these sacraments, though I see these three working together as a narrative. They tell a story of Christ's redemption and our living out and into a particular

---

1. I recognize that including confession as a sacrament will raise some eyebrows, though so will using the term sacrament in the first place. However, in the final chapter, I will offer a short excursus defending confession as a sacrament as well as defending what Hans Boersma calls a "sacramental ontology."

PART 3 | A SACRAMENTAL IDENTITY

identity, that of the Christian identity. I will argue that these sacraments and our participation in the liturgy in which they are received allow us to participate in the drama of Scripture and our identities which are, in fact, "in Christ" but more robustly than that of the modern formulations of that term and model. That is, there is sacramental participation in our future identity to which we are being transformed as we participate in the Holy Mysteries of the church.

5

Identity in the Great Tradition

Before setting out my constructive account of an identity shaped by and stabilized in the sacraments of the church, I would like to go back to history and look at three figures and their writings on the sacraments that I will cover in the final chapter. In this chapter, I will look at Saint Ambrose of Milan and his work *De Isaac* which was preached "to his catechumens (including, possibly, Augustine), either preparing for or recently having received baptism";[1] and Christina Rossetti and her eucharistic poetry, as well as her work *The Face of the Deep*. Finally, I will examine Saint Augustine of Hippo and his work *Confessions*. These authors and their writings covered in this penultimate chapter were pivotal for me in my understanding of the sacraments and their role in the shaping of one's identity. In the following pages, I will argue that these authors not only set out to write about the respective sacraments but also that they set out to show how these sacraments had shaped their identity and would do the same for any recipients of God's unique and sacramental grace in these holy mysteries.

BAPTISM IN SAINT AMBROSE OF MILAN

Saint Ambrose (ca. 340–397) was archbishop of Milan from 374 until his death. It was there, eleven years into his bishopric in Milan, that Ambrose and Augustine met. And this, perhaps, is what Ambrose is most notable for

---

1. Boersma, "Ambrose: Baptismal Identity and Human Identity," 169.

PART 3 | A SACRAMENTAL IDENTITY

his influence on Augustine, which can hardly be overstated.[2] During his time as bishop, Ambrose delivered many sermons that were later edited for publication. Many of these sermons have been determined to have either pre- or post-baptismal catechisms as their backdrop, his most famous being *On the Sacraments* and *On the Mysteries*. In another famous treatise, *On Repentance*, he has in mind repentance of sins committed after baptism and not with the repentance of conversion.[3] In fact, "the Ambrosian liturgy of the Church of Milan has a history as ancient and venerable as that of Rome, indeed, some scholars have held it to be the ancient Roman rite."[4] It is for these reasons that we turn to Ambrose specifically for our look at the understanding of baptism as identity within the Great Tradition.

Among Ambrose's baptismal sermons is one that many have found difficult to date and interpret: *De Isaac vel Anima* (*Isaac, or the Soul*).[5] Despite the text's difficulties, "scholarship is nearly unanimously agreed upon a baptismal context for the treatise."[6] Thus, whatever the dating, the oration is to be understood in light of its being preached to catechumens who are preparing for baptism or have just received baptism. However, more than just this, Gerald Boersma has persuasively argued that in Ambrose raising the question, "What, then, is man?" (*quid est . . . homo*),[7] he seeks to "articulate a baptismal anthropology. Baptism, for the Milanese bishop, profoundly reorients and fulfills human identity."[8]

Ambrose introduces the baptismal theme by first introducing us to the main characters of this work: Isaac and Rebecca. However, these characters and their story of meeting at the well in Gen 24 are to be understood in typological terms; Isaac points to Christ, and Rebecca points to the individual soul and/or the church. In his focus on these typological characters, we are introduced to the story, not of Rebecca coming to Isaac and the fountain to fill her water jar, but rather of the church coming to Christ and the well for a jar of water. In this reading of Gen 24, Ambrose is able to bring the text into conversation with both the Samaritan woman at the

---

2. For an excellent historical overview of the meeting of these two saints and Ambrose's influence on Augustine, see Brown, *Augustine of Hippo*, 69–78.

3. Ferguson, *Baptism in the Early Church*, 635.

4. Mitchell, "Ambrosian Baptismal Rites," 241–53.

5. Boersma, "Ambrose: Baptismal Identity and Human Identity," 168–91.

6. Boersma, "Ambrose: Baptismal Identity and Human Identity," 169.

7. Ambrose, *De Isaac*, 2.3.

8. Boersma, "Ambrose: Baptismal Identity and Human Identity," 168.

well in John 4 and the bridal language of the Song of Songs. It is this image of the soul/the church coming to Christ as one seeking an eternal drink of living water to which Ambrose's catechumens can immediately relate as they prepare for their journey to this same fountain.

The oration quickly turns away from the text of Genesis and moves into an extended discussion of the Song of Songs as a fuller picture of the soul's/church's union with Christ. Ambrose is mainly taken by the bride's desirous words, "Let him kiss me with the kisses of his mouth!" (Song 1:2). Commenting on this verse, Ambrose writes, "Such a soul also desires many kisses of the Word, so that she may be enlightened with the light of the knowledge of God. For this is the kiss of the Word . . . God the Word kisses us, when he enlightens our heart and governing faculty with the spirit of the knowledge of God."[9] Boersma explains how this "kiss of the Word" and "enlightenment" link is made "so that the 'kiss' becomes a dominant metaphor for baptism."[10] Thus Ambrose sees the sacrament of the baptismal kiss as that moment in which the soul is united with Christ.

It seems that this personal exegesis of the Song (as opposed to the ecclesial interpretation) is the predominant occupation of Ambrose's oration, for he is concerned with why the bride of the Song is "black but lovely" (Song 1:5 NASB). Ambrose finds his answer later, stating, "she has been darkened by her union with the body."[11] Hans Boersma sums it up well, "Ambrose very much wants the bride to overcome the bodily passions, leave behind the lust of the body, and learn to resist the temptations of the world."[12] Indeed, as G. Boersma indicates, "Ambrose . . . appears to be developing a baptismal anthropology, and in doing so, he lists his negative evaluation of the body to its post-lapsarian state."[13] That is, "Ambrose treats the body with suspicion only in its fallen state (after the fall and prior to baptism)."[14] Quoting Ambrose at length will prove useful here:

> Now she is not aware of the remnants of the flesh; now, like a spirit, she has divested herself of the connection with the body; now, as if she had forgotten and could not remember their union even if she wished, she says, "I have taken off my robe, how shall I put it

9. Ambrose, *De Isaac*, 3.8.
10. Boersma, "Ambrose: Baptismal Identity and Human Identity," 180.
11. Ambrose, *De Isaac*, 4.13.
12. H. Boersma, *Scripture as Real Presence*, 213.
13. Boersma, "Ambrose: Baptismal Identity and Human Identity," 177.
14. Boersma, "Ambrose: Baptismal Identity and Human Identity," 177.

on?" For she took off that robe of skins which Adam and Eve had received after their sin, the robe of corruption, the robe of the passions. "How shall I put it on?" She does not seek again to put it on, but by this she means that it has been thrown away, so that it cannot now be her covering. "I have washed my feet, how shall I defile them?"; that is, I have washed my feet, to go forth and lift myself up from association with the body; "how shall I defile them?" to return to the enclosure of the body and the gloomy prison of its passions?[15]

A few things are important to note in this section. As G. Boersma noted, Ambrose has in mind the corruption of the body in a post-lapsarian state, the "robe of skins which Adam and Eve had received *after* their sin."[16] This cuts across a common misunderstanding that what we have in Ambrose and other fathers of the church is a capitulation to Greek philosophy that disparages the body entirely as "the well-known Platonic description of the body as the 'prison house' from which the soul ought to escape."[17]

The section also further indicates the baptismal context of *De Isaac vel Anima* by his mention and interpretation of the woman's words in Song 5:3. A known distinctive in the Ambrosian baptismal rite is that of a foot washing that took place after the baptism and the anointing of the head by the bishop.[18] Additionally, the early church tradition included being baptized naked and clothed in white robes after the baptism, which indicated Paul's reference to putting off the old man and putting on the new (Eph 4:22–24).[19] Furthermore, Ambrose's focus on one's putting on of the new man and the nuptial context of Song of Songs in which the woman cannot possibly go back to the old robes or defile her newly sanctified feet as she has bound herself to Christ shows that Ambrose has in mind here a baptismal anthropology in which our identity has been shaped and made new by the sacrament. This leads me to a slight departure from the focus of the work of Gerald Boersma.

15. Ambrose, *De Isaac*, 6.52.
16 Ambrose, *De Isaac*, 6.52 (emphasis added).
17. Boersma, "Ambrose: Baptismal Identity and Human Identity," 177.
18. Ferguson, *Baptism in the Early Church*, 639.
19. See Ambrose, "Mysteries," 7.34.

It should be noted that the tradition of baptismal clothing is near-universal and considered to be an apostolic tradition, whereas the post-baptismal foot washing was an Ambrosian distinctive and one that did not have any legs, so to speak (bad pun, unfortunately, intended).

IDENTITY IN THE GREAT TRADITION

Whereas I agree with the assessment of the baptismal identity as the unifying theme in *De Isaac*, I want to focus on the conclusion of Ambrose and the ecclesial context that this inevitably brings the treatise. Hans Boersma reads this treatise in line with Karl Shuve, who says, "Ambrose is thoroughly preoccupied with the ascetic renunciation of the body, which marks his exegesis at every turn."[20] And while Hans Boersma even states that "it is the personal exegesis of the Song that really matters to Ambrose," he continues by adding that "it is the church (and in baptism) that the soul obtains her true identity."[21] Ambrose seems more likely to see baptism and this new identity intimately connected with the mystical union of one's soul to a new body, the body of Christ. So it is not by the *renunciation* of the body by which the bride overcomes but by the *pronouncement* of a new body to which her soul clings.

In his later work "The Mysteries," Ambrose continues his reflections on the Song for the sake of baptismal catechesis. In his comments on Song 1:5 ("I am black but beautiful") he states, "black through the frailty of human condition, beautiful through grace; black, because I am made up of sinners, beautiful by the sacrament of faith."[22] Ambrose flows in and out of the individual and ecclesial reading of the "black but beautiful" bride. She is the church that is darkened by her incorporation of individual sinners who are darkened by their own sinful passions. Ambrose instructs his catechumens on what takes place in the waters of baptism as they drink from this fount of living water. This water gives new life. It gives them a new identity and a new body as they are welcomed into the church, the body of Christ. No longer is the bride "black but lovely." Instead, she is "in all her glory, having no spot or wrinkle" (Eph 5:27 NASB). Both the individual soul and the bridal body of Christ are made new by the nuptial vows of the sacrament of baptism as she is "washed by the water of the Word" (Eph 5:26) and now "clothed always in white" (Eccl 9:8).[23] Her cry "Let him kiss me with the kisses of his mouth" (Song 1:2) is met by the King as he draws her in. This is where Ambrose moves to the great mystery of the Eucharist, the marriage supper to which the King ushers in his newly washed Bride. Here he comments on Song 4:10, "Christ then feeds His Church on these

---

20 Shuve, *Song of Songs and the Fashioning of Identity*, 138.

21. H. Boersma, *Scripture as Real Presence*, 212–13.

22. Ambrose, "Mysteries," 7.35.

23. See ACCS for baptismal readings of this text in the interpretive tradition of the early church.

sacraments, by which the substance of the soul is made strong, and, seeing the continuous advancement of her grace, rightly says to her: 'How beautiful thy breasts have become, my sister, my spouse, how beautiful they have become from wine.'"[24] It is to this marriage supper of the Eucharist that we now turn. And for our look at this sacrament we will look to a very different guide, the nineteenth century Anglo-Catholic poet Christina Rossetti.

THE EUCHARIST IN CHRISTINA ROSSETTI[25]

The female English author of romantic, devotional, liturgically oriented, and children's poems, Christina Rossetti (1830–94) began writing at an early age and published numerous books of collected poems and became one of the greatest poets of her time. However, despite the brilliance of her scripturally saturated work, scant scholarly attention has been paid from the church. This becomes increasingly peculiar as we understand her relationship with the Oxford Movement. It has long been understood that perhaps the biggest influence on her poetry and prose was that of the Tractarian influence. The Anglo-Catholic movement of the Church of England in which she, her mother, and her sister became heavily involved came at an important time for Rossetti. Her father was extremely ill and unable to work while Christina was still young, and the rest of her family had begun to do what they could to help their mother provide for the family, which resulted in feelings of isolation and depression. This involvement with the church seems to have helped as it thrust her into a new community—a point and theme throughout her poetry, which we will explore further below. Two major themes or elements of Rossetti's poetry will be particularly important for my purposes here: the sacramental character and worldview that seems to undergird her interpretation and the theme of the communion of the saints. The former will be shown in our exploration of the latter, as the sacramental nature and theme shows itself as more of a particular quality or characteristic of her writing. This is particularly true in her typological use of language and interpretation of Scripture.[26]

---

24. Ambrose, "Mysteries," 9.55.

25. The following section is indebted to the works of Ludlow: "Christina Rossetti: Identity in the Communion of Saints," 543–53 (hereafter "Identity in the Communion of Saints"); and *Christina Rossetti and the Bible: Waiting with the Saints* (hereafter *Waiting with the Saints*).

26. For a sacramental description and understanding of typological and allegorical

IDENTITY IN THE GREAT TRADITION

Elizabeth Ludlow, professor of English literature at Anglia Ruskin University, in her article entitled "Christina Rossetti: Identity in the Communion of the Saints," seeks to read Rossetti in light of her historical context, "a time when the martyrs of the ancient and medieval world were an object of religious and literary scrutiny."[27] Ludlow makes keen observations in Rossetti's poetry based on her statement that "one who cannot be martyr in deed may yet be martyr in will,"[28] arguing that this recognition "forms the root of her understanding of the foundation of Christian identity."[29] Ludlow then connects this recognition to a eucharistic focus in Rossetti's poetry, where one finds themselves most visibly in the communion of the saints: past, present, and future.

This focus in Rossetti's words is seen most clearly in the content and structure of her work "Martyrs' Song." The first stanza alerts us to the voices of the martyrs of Christ: "We meet in joy, tho' we part in sorrow; We part tonight, but we meet tomorrow."[30] As the poem continues the voices heard throughout broaden out and include not just those who have parted through death but all the saints. Ludlow points out how Rossetti begins to draw on the book of Hebrews and "the new and living way" that Jesus "opened for us through the curtain, that is, through his flesh" (Heb 10:20). Rossetti therefore is drawing on the invitation and exhortation of that chapter to not neglect meeting together as the day draws near (10:25). That is to say, this language in Rossetti's poem evokes the communion of the saints and invites the readers into it.[31] Furthermore, it was this invitation and entrance into communion that radically shapes one's identity. This is because to be a martyr in deed or in will is to "un-self" one's self.[32] That is, to be a martyr is to be so marked by Christ crucified, his kingdom, and his people that "it is no longer I who live, but Christ who lives in me" (Gal 2:20).

From here, Ludlow continues to demonstrate how a close reading of Rossetti's work and an understanding of her own Anglo-Catholic tradition shows that Rossetti agreed with the church that "the Eucharist is the site where fellowship with Christ and with the church, as the 'body of Christ,' is

---

readings of Scripture and use of language, see Boersma, *Scripture as Real Presence*.

27. Ludlow, "Identity in the Communion of Saints," 543.
28. Rossetti, *Face of the Deep*, 465.
29. Ludlow, "Identity in the Communion of Saints," 543.
30. Rossetti, *Complete Poems*, 76 (hereafter cited as *CP*).
31. Ludlow, "Identity in the Communion of Saints," 546.
32. Williams, *Wound of Knowledge*, 27.

expressed most visibly."³³ Her poems use much eucharistic language. "Martyrs' Song" states in the fifth stanza:

> God the Father give us grace
> To walk in the light of Jesus' Face.
> God the Son give us a part
> In the hiding-place of Jesus' Heart:
> God the Spirit so hold us up
> That we may drink of Jesus' cup.³⁴

Thus, in line with the aforementioned arrangement and theme of this poem, it appears that Rossetti is reflecting on Jesus' cup, praying that she might be upheld so that she might drink and so be unified to the saints.

Elsewhere, Ludlow makes use of Rossetti's poem "A Better Resurrection." In this devotional poem she indicates a life that is empty but for which hope is found in being made a sacrifice to the Lord:

> My life is like a broken bowl
> A broken bowl that cannot hold
> One drop of water for my soul
> Or cordial in the searching cold;
> Cast in the fire the perished thing,
> Melt and remould it, till it be
> A royal cup for Him my King:
> O Jesus, drink of me!³⁵

These lines portray the painful hope of the "un-selfing" mentioned above. As Ludlow writes, "The speaker's recognition of her own brokenness and alienation can best be understood in the context of the economy of martyrdom."³⁶ Framed in our own conversation, these lines are, in many ways, cries about her own identity and a desire to be recast as someone caught up in that communion of the saints, honoring the King with her life as a sacrifice. However, it must not be missed that the final line emphasizes that the setting of this self-offering is the Lord's Table.

Finally, I want to look at Rossetti's final publication in 1893, published just one year prior to her death. *Verses* is the only collection of Rossetti's to contain religious poetry alone.³⁷ I am particularly interested in highlighting

33. Ludlow, "Identity in the Communion of Saints," 551.
34. Rossetti, CP, 176.
35. Rossetti, CP, 62.
36. Ludlow, "Identity in the Communion of Saints," 552.
37. Dieleman, *Religious Imaginaries*, 137.

IDENTITY IN THE GREAT TRADITION

this work due to its nature as a collection of strictly religious work from the past, as she recognizes the closeness of her death as she suffered much in the last years of her life. Her interest in reflecting on the subjects of the cross, salvation, the sacraments—particularly the Eucharist—and the communion of the saints is no coincidence. Death is a moment when many face existential questions and crises; Rossetti turned to the one thing that can give one comfort: Christ and the sacraments, which unite us to him and his church and point us toward the sure hope of resurrection.

We see something of these thoughts on death and the hope of resurrection in "Judge not according to the appearance."

> Lord, purge our eyes to see
> Within the seed a tree,
> Within the glowing egg a bird,
> Within the shroud a butterfly:
>
> Till taught by such, we see
> Beyond all creatures Thee,
> And hearken for Thy tender word,
> And hear it,"Fear not: it is I."[38]

These two stanzas have images of new life coming out of the shrouds of darkness. A seed burrowed deep in the ground, a bird in the darkness of its egg, a caterpillar that springs to a new life as a butterfly out of the dark tomb of its cocoon. Such a theme evokes the greatest moment of new life from a tomb, that of the resurrected Christ. This moment of the resurrection of Jesus, however, is significant beyond his own personal resurrection as it signals the defeat of death and the tomb, as the new life he offers to all is possible because of his death alone.[39] However, the poem starts as a prayer

---

38. Rossetti, *CP*, 418.

39. Furthermore, I want to note that it is particularly interesting that one of the most notable narratives of Jesus' resurrection comes in Luke 24, where the disciples' vision seems to be impaired or veiled as they do not recognize the resurrected Christ. However, it is the moment they are breaking bread in verses 30–31 that the veil is lifted, and they recognize Jesus as the man they have been walking and talking with. Moreover, in the narrative, they also recognize him in all the Scriptures, and though it is not explicit in this text, I believe we should understand verses 30–31 as implying that they recognized him in the blessed and broken bread. That is, in a eucharistic way. Indeed, Christ did make it explicit in the Last Supper and elsewhere in his recorded teachings, such as John 6:22–59.

All this to say, it does not seem coincidental that Rossetti has combined these themes of life in death and a sacramental vision in this way. This is another way she seems to evoke echoes of the Eucharist in her poetry.

to the Lord to teach her, to teach us all, to see. Even the imagery of this new sight that we wish the Lord to grant us is a new spiritual sight that comes out of the riddance, the death, of our old ways of seeing. This new vision she seeks is that of a sacramental one that sees through and past the mere natural elements of this world and sees the greater realities in which they participate. The ultimate reality, however, which she points to in the second stanza, is that of Christ: "beyond all creatures Thee." She seeks to be formed so that she sees Christ as in all. To truly see that, as Paul states in Acts 17, it is "in Him" we and all other creatures "live and move and have our being" (Acts 17:28).

Further, the two-stanza which we just looked at falls as one of the final four poems of a collection within *Verses* titled, "Christ, Our All in All" and in the penultimate poem of this collection, "A chill blank world. Yet over the utmost sea." She again writes of the impending death that we all face, but which she most assuredly feels as her closest companion: "A chill blank world. Yet over the utmost sea. The light of a coming dawn is rising to me." Though she faces death, it seems that something of that sacramental vision has been given to her, and she can see the coming dawn of that resurrection life which awaits her. More importantly, this hope is not just found within herself. No, she draws from the hopeful words of the liturgy. She alludes to the Sursum Corda of the eucharistic liturgy found in the *Book of Common Prayer*, which begins the liturgy of the table.

> Priest: Lift up your hearts
> Answer: We lift them up unto the Lord.
> Priest: Let us give thanks unto our Lord God.
> Answer: It is meet and right so to do.[40]

We see her drawing and pointing to the liturgy two lines later: "While I lift my heart, O Lord, my heart unto thee." It seems that the mention of the Sursum Corda is an example of metalepsis.[41] She looks to bring in the whole of the eucharistic liturgy by alluding to this line. In carrying the eucharistic liturgy into the background, she draws in the sacrament itself and the communion of the saints with which we participate in that

---

40. Bray and Keane, *1662 Book of Common Prayer*.

41. "The term metalepsis has been connected in the history of rhetoric to metonymy, a figure of speech often described as a part standing in for the whole. Using this association, we can understand metalepsis as an author's reference to the larger literary context when offering a citation or allusion from an earlier text. In this sense, *metalepsis* is the use of a part of a precursor text to evoke the whole of it" (Brown, "Metalepsis," 30).

sacrament.⁴² That is, we do not lift up our hearts alone, take the sacrament alone, nor enter into death or new resurrection life alone. Even though the language used in the poem is that of the first-person singular, she alludes to the liturgy, which is always spoken in the first-person plural.

This brings us to the final poem in the collection: "The chiefest among ten thousand." Here, she begins with a citation of Song 5:10. As we saw in the section on Saint Ambrose, the Song is seen allegorically as a Song that refers to Christ and his bride, the church. Furthermore, we also saw how the early church understood the song in liturgical contexts, especially as it spoke to the sacraments of baptism and the Eucharist. Chapter 5 of the Song specifically speaks of the bride's search for her beloved. The anticipation is built as the bride, in a dream-like state (v. 2), hears the bridegroom coming and opens the door only to be disappointed by his absence (vv. 5–6). The rest of the Song consists of the bride's praises and adoration and longing to be present with the bridegroom, a resolve that doesn't take place until chapter 6 of the Song. Rossetti has opened this final poem of the collection with a line from the Song because it, too, awaits the Bridegroom, the King: Jesus. Rossetti waits for Jesus' final, kingly entry saying:

> Palm branch its triumph, harp uplifts
> Its triumph-note melodious:

In this, one of her last poems ever published, Rossetti awaits the coming of her King, her bridegroom. Whereas, as we have seen throughout her poetry, Rossetti has most consistently spoken of her communion with the saints, she now, at the end of her life, most awaits her communion with Christ himself:

> O, Jesu, better than Thy saints
> Art Thou Thine only self to us!⁴³

Furthermore, it is certain that Rossetti read the Song in such a way of evoking the relationship of King Jesus and his church as his bride when

---

42. It is important to note that Rossetti has explicitly made use of the Sursum Corda in a short poem entitled Sursum Corda, which begins:
"Lift up your hearts." "We lift them up." Ah me!
(Rossetti, CP, 519)
I say this to note that it is not a stretch to see Rossetti's use here as a reference toward the liturgy. I have not made use of this explicit work, however, due to my interest in Rossetti's reference to the liturgy within the theme of death in "A Chill Blank World" and its overall place in her particular collection and the way these poems come together.

43. Rossetti, CP, 419.

she makes mention of the Song in her commentary on Revelation, *The Face of the Deep*. In her comments on Rev 19:7 she focuses on "the marriage of the Lamb is come, and His wife hath made herself ready." To do this, she surveys the narrative of Scripture by the mention of all the brides that God brought to their bridegrooms as a type of the church being called to Christ: "As God brought Eve to Adam, so now is He bringing each pure and lovely soul to Christ." In the list, which spans nearly two pages, she mentions these many characters of Scripture by name and something of an historical marker or narrative detail. However, her allusions to the Song come only twice in the entire section on Rev 19:7 and in very different ways: both in the forms of citation, as though the book is the foundation for such a figurative or sacramental reading of these OT narratives. That is, the Song of Songs provides the scriptural and theological basis on which she is able to read all marriages of the Bible as sacramentally participating in the true and ultimate marriage of Christ and the church of which the verse in Revelation is speaking. The first citation of the Song comes near the beginning of this short biblical theology of marriage, saying, "As the daughters of Zelophehad were espoused by their near kinsmen, so to blessed souls Christ deigns to say, 'My sister, My spouse.'"[44] The second citation closes the entire section on this verse of Revelation:

> She has come up from the wildness leaning upon her Beloved, and leaning upon Him she will sit down in the Promised Land flowing with milk and honey.
> "The Voice of my Beloved! . . . Arise, My love, My fair one, and come away."[45]

Rossetti, ever the poet and skilled master of the art of style in written text, places her words in no accidental form. The words with which this section opens are a quotation of the verse in question, Rev 19:7, a text that speaks of the marriage of the Lamb which has come and in which the Bride has now made herself ready. In master style, the verse with which Rossetti closes this section is a quotation of a different verse, though it is one that still speaks to the marriage of the Lamb; however, now that the Bride has herself ready (Rev 19:7), the bridegroom now calls, "Arise . . . Come away" (Song 2:10).

---

44. Rossetti, *Face of the Deep*, 433, citing Song 4:9, 10, 12, and 5:1.
45. Rossetti, *Face of the Deep*, 436, citing Song 2:10.

Christina Rossetti longed to be a "martyr in will." That is, she longed to be a *witness* of Christ and the gospel of his death and resurrection. This longing, this mission of hers, marked her identity from a young age, and as her consistent echoes of the eucharistic liturgy show, she believed this to be enacted each week at the altar of the blessed sacrament. It was there that, though she could not be "a martyr in deed" by truly dying for the gospel and mission of Christ, she was "a martyr in will" dying to herself in Christ. The Eucharist shaped and formed her identity as a martyr, a witness for Christ. What Rossetti shows us is that the Holy Mystery of the Eucharist marks and shapes our life and our death. As we participate in this blessed sacrament we are formed in our life as we prepare for our death. Therefore, the sacrament forms our life until the end. Rossetti's life and poetry are a witness to the identity-shaping power of the Eucharist as it carried her until the final days, where she cries, "Forget not my life, O my Lord, forget not my death."[46]

In closing this section on the poetry of Christina Rossetti, I believe that Ludlow sums up well in saying that, throughout Rossetti, we find that "all identity is centered around and in Christ." However, I would adjust this slightly in saying that while this is true to some degree, it misses a key element throughout Rossetti's poetry which sees this via one's self being caught up in the liturgy of the church, the sacraments of the church, and the communion of the saints of the past, present, and future; that is, the *body* of Christ. Therefore, we might rightly say that "Rossetti's poetry offers a challenge that carries a particular resonance at a time when individuality is prioritized over community."[47]

CONFESSION IN SAINT AUGUSTINE OF HIPPO

Among Saint Augustine's most well-known works is his autobiographical *Confessions*, written sometime between 397 and 401. The first nine books of the work consist primarily of autobiography, while books 10 to 13 dive into what seems like a strangely placed theological treatise on time, memory, and the creation narratives of Genesis. This topical analysis of the work and the seemingly disjointed nature of books 10 to 13 has kept scholars of Augustine busy for a long time. However, it is the very relations between these two sections of the work that I am interested in here for the purposes

---

46. Rossetti, *CP*, 418.
47. Ludlow, "Identity in the Communion of Saints," 553.

of a theology of identity. Augustine's posited relationship between narrative, time, memory, and the sacrament of confession creates a foundational groundwork for the theology of identity that I am proposing here. Furthermore, though the saint may not have used such language, it is clear that in these final books, he understands confession—what he has just done in books 1 to 9 of *Confessions*—as formational for a person's relationship to God, to the church, and ultimately for the human person, their self: their identity.

In James K. A. Smith's incisive work *On the Road with Saint Augustine*, we are given a different look at the Bishop of Hippo, one that Smith describes in his introduction as more like an "AA sponsor,"[48] an Augustine who's read alongside French existentialists like Sartre and Camus or phenomenologists like Heidegger. However, it is the Augustine that Smith discusses as a fellow traveler on the road, one familiar with the twists and turns, the difficulties, and the detours of the journey of life that I am interested in here. This is because *this* Augustine recognizes that this road is formational and is an intimate part of who you are. Those who seek authenticity and claim this form of expression as their true self know the road well. However, for them, the road is not just the road. The road is home. Augustine understands this all too well, but of the bishop's many confessions, his greatest and most important is the one found early in his story when he says to God, "our heart is restless until it rests in you."[49] Augustine knows the road well, but the greatest thing he learned while on the road is that the road can *never* be home but *leads* to our true home in resting in the presence of our creator and that this home is a place where we will truly one day arrive. This is a point he drives home in another of his memorable statements, "I would learn to discern and distinguish the difference . . . between those who see what the goal is but not how to get there and those who see the way which leads to the home of bliss, not merely as an end to be perceived but as a realm to live in."[50] Yet, it is important to remember and read Augustine rightly here. Augustine is not one to scoff at the journey. He recognizes that the road forms us; it is a part of who we are, and we bring our whole selves with us when we arrive at our destination. In fact, in some

---

48. Smith, *On the Road with Saint Augustine*, xi. The following section is indebted to Smith's insightful and often poetic work.

49. Augustine, *Conf.* I.i.1 (unless otherwise noted, all quotes are from the Chadwick translation).

50. Augustine, *Conf.* VII.xx.26.

IDENTITY IN THE GREAT TRADITION

ways, Augustine might even say that our memory of ourselves on the road to the present *is* who we are.

> Great is the power of memory, an awe-inspiring mystery, my God, a power of profound and infinite multiplicity. And this is mind, this is I myself. What then am I, my God? What is my nature? It is characterized by diversity, by life of many forms, utterly immeasurable. See the broad plains and caves and caverns of my memory. The varieties there cannot be counted, and are, beyond any reckoning, full of innumerable things.[51]

But what about who we are in the present? Doesn't this matter all the more? The authenticity model might say that whoever we are now—whatever decisions in the past might have brought us where we are—is the most true version of who we are. The changes and life "characterized by diversity" and "by life of many forms"[52] have only brought us to where we are, which is our most authentic selves. However, Augustine would see that as a misunderstanding of the relationship between the past, the present, and memory:

> If future and past events exist, I want to know where they are. If I have not the strength to discover the answer, at least I know that wherever they are, they are not there as future or past, but as present. For if there also they are future, they will not yet be there. If there also they are past, they are no longer there. Therefore, wherever they are, whatever they are, they do not exist except in the present. When a true narrative of the past is related, the memory produces not the actual events which have passed away but words conceived from images of them, which they fixed in the mind like imprints as they passed through the senses. Thus my boyhood, which is no longer, lies in past time which is no longer. But when I am recollecting and telling my story, I am looking on its image in present time, since it is still in my memory.[53]

The present is the only place where the past even exists through memory. Brian L. Horne comments on the passage, "The strange possibility presents itself that the only thing that is real is the memory. Considered from the perspective of time passing, no process can have meaning, nothing can be known, until it is completed and thus remembered from the standpoint of

---

51. Augustine, *Conf.* X.xvii.26.

52. Or as the R. S. Pine-Coffin translation says, "A life that ever varying, full of change, and of immense power."

53. Augustine, *Conf.* XI.xviii.23.

the end of time. The astonishing closing chapters (27–31) make this point over and over again."⁵⁴

And herein lies Augustine's connection between these two sections of *Confessions*. Augustine writes as one who presently stands on the road with a newfound outlook on the journey taken and the destination. However, Augustine's own claim for the purpose of his work is that it is by looking at the road behind us with the transformed vision of God's grace that we can have a right understanding of where our home is and the formative purpose of the road that still lies before us. In his essay "'A Question to Myself': Time and Self-Awareness in the *Confessions*," the former archbishop of Canterbury Rowan Williams reflects on how Augustine ties this to the narrative of the gospel and the incarnation:

> The ascent to heaven is first a descent to our earth; as with Christ, so with us. . . . The question of who or what exactly I am, the nature of self or soul, is to be understood in relation to the story of Christ's acceptance of the weakness of mortality. If my identity is determined by the inaccessible but unfailing attention of God's love, the incarnation of the divine Word in Jesus is a declaration that this divine attention is in touch with us and transforming us through a particular worldly series of events transmitted by human telling, active in the present through the historical body of the Church. . . . I am changed only when I begin to follow the path of Christ and, by grace, to shape a biography of my own that conforms to the contours of his, embracing mortality and limit in order to receive a life beyond mortality and limit.⁵⁵

For Augustine, embracing the hope of the narrative of Christ and the church requires the confession and embrace of the narrative of their past and present need for the hopeful future.

It is for this reason that Augustine has been seen as the originator of narrative identity: "Though we may not be able to ascribe to Augustine the genesis of the modern notion of personhood, we can infer from his introduction to the genre of autobiographical literature that Augustine placed an original emphasis upon the value of the storied-self."⁵⁶ This is particularly spelled out in book 10 of *Confessions*, where he opens with, "May I know you who know me. May I 'know as I also am known' (1 Cor. 13:12). Power

---

54. Horne, "Person as Confession," 72.
55. Williams, *On Augustine*, 12.
56. DeLashmutt, "Paul Ricoeur at the Foot of the Cross," 599.

of my soul, enter into it and fit it for yourself, so that you may have it and hold it 'without spot or blemish' (Eph. 5:27). This is my hope, and that is why I speak. In this hope I am placing my delight when my delight is in what it ought to be."[57] This book comes at the end of the "autobiographical" section of *Confessions*, which he begins in book 1 with a confession of God's lordship and reflects on the fact that to call upon God and come to know him is to be humbled and to know yourself.[58] That is, to come to know God, the one who truly knows you, is to understand yourself better because you come to know the you that God created and formed, the real you!

On Pears, Job, Friends, and Confession

Near the beginning of *Confessions*, Saint Augustine tells a story that is arguably the most well-known portion of the entire work. We are told of when Augustine, with his friends, needlessly stole some pears. Augustine reflects deeply on what is seemingly a rather innocuous sin:

> What fruit did I, wretched man, derive from these things, which I now blush to recall, particularly in that act of theft, in which I loved the theft itself and nothing else, since it was itself nothing and I became more wretched through it? Yet, I would not have done it by myself (that is my recollection of my mind at the time); I certainly would not have done it alone. Therefore, I also loved in it the companionship of those with whom I did it.[59]

Shortly before this, Augustine has already hinted at the desire that had been in him to please and find common ground with his peers:

> I went rashly along in such blindness that I was ashamed to be less wanton than my contemporaries, for I used to hear them boasting about their shameful exploits. The more evil these youths were, the more they boasted, and I was pleased not only by the evil pleasure of action but by the pleasure of boasting. What but vice is deserving of vituperation? I became more vicious, so that I would not be

---

57. Augustine, *Conf.* X.i.1.

58. We see how this influenced the later John Calvin, who opens his *Institutes of the Christian Religion* with the first section titled "Without knowledge of self there is no knowledge of God" and opens with the statement, "Nearly all the wisdom we possess, that is to say, true and sound wisdom, consists of two parts: the knowledge of God and of ourselves. But, while joined by many bonds, which one precedes and brings forth the other is not easy to discern" (Calvin, *Institutes* I.1).

59. Augustine, *Conf*, 2.8.16.

vituperated and, when my conduct did not match the wickedness of my associates, I pretended to have perpetrated deeds which I had not performed, lest I would appear inferior because I was more innocent, lest I be considered viler because I was more chaste.[60]

From these two excerpts of Augustine's most personal work we see that he was no stranger to the yearning to know and be known, no stranger to the desire for companionship. It seems that Augustine's understanding of himself and self-expression were being affected by his choice of companionship, and Augustine was aware of how these negatives were shaping him.[61] He's caught by this dilemma wherein he thought he might better understand himself through the ones who know him best. Yet, this led him to become dishonest about himself; he presented a false self out of a desire to feel known. The irony is rich.

Yet, we know from elsewhere in this personal account of his own life that there was an inner turmoil within him. Earlier Augustine had spoken highly of things which he had found within himself, which he knew to be "the gifts of my God,"[62] saying:

> I had the power of sensing. I was concerned about my well-being ... I took care of the integrity of my senses by means of my interior sense. I delighted in truth ... I did not want to be mistaken; I developed a good memory; I learned to speak well; I was consoled by friendship; I fled from suffering, dejection, and ignorance. Is it not wonderful and praiseworthy to be endowed with such life?[63]

However, Augustine continues, "But in this I sinned: I sought enjoyments, honors, and truths, not in Him but in His creatures, myself and others."[64] As R. S. Pine-Coffin's translation so aptly notes, Augustine believed, "My inner self was a house divided against itself."[65] This division is profoundly recognized in the comparison between the confessions of book 1, that our hearts are restless until they find rest in God and that "I would have no

---

60. Augustine, *Conf.* 2.3.7.

61. It is important to note that Augustine goes to great pains to make it clear, particularly in the story of the pears, that his sinfulness is not the fault of his community. He recognizes a bit of a paradox that it is his own depravity that draws him to the sin, yet it is also for the sake of companionship.

62. Augustine, *Conf.* 1.20.

63. Augustine, *Conf.* 1.20.

64. Augustine, *Conf.* 1.20.

65. Augustine, *Conf.* 8.8 (Pine-Coffin trans., 170).

being, I would not have any existence, unless you were in me,"⁶⁶ and the story which we just read in book 2 wherein Augustine seeks to find rest and being in the knowledge and companionship of his friends.

I want to quickly compare this to another story of a man who found himself caught in the turmoil of self-knowledge and the companionship of friends and their third-person knowledge. In the story of Job we begin with a strange behind-the-scenes look at what is to come, a heavenly scene in which Satan comes before the presence of God and we are let in on a back-and-forth about the uprightness of the man Job. God tells Satan "that there is none like him on the earth, a blameless and upright man, who fears God and turns away from evil" (Job 1:8). Satan's response is that this is only true because God has made it easy for Job, but if God were to curse him and his possessions, Job would curse God in return. Now, of the many theological and exegetical difficulties that a text like this may contain, I must leave it to the experts. However, I do want to note that the statement from the Lord about Job shows his knowledge about the character of Job, his creature, his "servant." Throughout the story, we are let in on conversations between Job and those who should know him best. His wife tells him to finally just let go of his integrity and to "curse God and die" (2:9). Most of the rest of the book is filled with these long diatribes from Job's friends and his responses to them as they try to offer Job their wisdom about the situation. However, what we find in 42:7–9 is a rebuke of Job's friends by God, for they have not offered wisdom but foolishness, and they have not spoken truthfully about God or Job. In fact, in two of these three verses, God makes it a point that Job spoke rightly of who God is, but Job's friends did not. However, just before God's rebuke, we are shown that it is Job's knowledge of God and his character that brings him to his long-sought understanding of himself, which his friends (who did not know God rightly) could not offer (42:1–6). Job discovers the ultimate truth of who God is and who he himself is: God is the creator, and Job is created; he is "dust and ashes" (42:6; compare Gen 18:27).

I insert this narrative here because it offers a biblical mirror to Augustine's understanding of his dilemma regarding his friends and their knowledge of him as opposed to God and his knowledge of Augustine. Though it may seem that those around us know us best and can speak to who we are, there is always the One who knows us better. This is why Augustine would say our restless souls find rest only in God because—in the language of James K. A. Smith—we can find rest only in the place that our soul calls

---

66. Augustine, *Conf.* 1.2.2.

PART 3 | A SACRAMENTAL IDENTITY

home. As Augustine noted above, he sought "truths" in God's "creatures, himself, and others."[67] The road is winding and leads us home, but it is not home; it is not where we find the Truth. So where does the sacrament of confession come in?

Both Job and Augustine end the same, with confession. Confession is tricky because, as we will explore more fully in the next chapter, there is a two-fold nature of confession: (1) confession of sin or wrong-doing, which is a reflection of a past event, but also (2) it is a proclamation of a present reality, the confession that Christ is Lord and our only means of forgiveness and salvation. Confession of sins to Christ contains both: We confess that we have sinned against God, which, at the very least, implies that Christ is the sovereign Lord over our lives and that we are in the need of his redemption and saving grace. Augustine recognizes this, which is why he writes his treatise on time and memory at the end of his autobiographical reflections or confessions. Augustine's story focuses much on his past journey, his search for himself, and his search for God, and then moves into thoughts about the mystery of memory. He ends with confessions of God's timeless eternity and perfect knowledge. The connecting point is that Augustine views confession (the sacramental act in which he has just participated throughout the whole of his work) as God's invitation to his own timeless knowledge of who we are and how he sees us. Confession is where we *presently* reflect on the *past* so that we might come to know who we really are and who God is making us to be in the *future* through Christ.

---

67. Augustine, *Conf.* 1.20.

6

Sacramental Identity

THE MODELS OF IDENTITY offered to us at this point have within them inherent flaws that must be answered. In tracing both the "authenticity" model and the "in-Christ" model, I have sought to show how we are in need of a new understanding of personal identity and identity formation. Our theological anthropology is in need of a theologically robust model of personality identity. Such a model must emphasize the transformation of the Holy Spirit through our union with Christ without deeming embodied particularities or narratively indexed aspects of identity as useless or unimportant. This emphasis must be sustained while also offering a grounding component that stabilizes[1] identity through the narratival changes which occur through time.

Throughout this chapter, my contention is that such a model must be thoroughly ecclesiological and sacramental. An ecclesiological model keeps us from the modern tendency of an isolated and individualistic understanding of the authenticity model. My model will also seek to further elaborate on the "in Christ" language throughout Scripture by showing how this union with Christ is to be seen, in part, through our incorporation into the *body* of Christ. By focusing on the ecclesial *body* of Christ we not only avoid the danger of diminishing the narratively indexed aspects of identity, but they are, in fact, highlighted as adding greater value to the body of Christ through the diversity of its members. Furthermore, such a

---

1. By "stabilizing" I mean the process of grounding our identity in something of a fixed state through the changes which have occurred in our past and which will inevitably occur in the future that narratively index and shape or form our identity.

model, rooted in the sacraments as it is, avoids the dangers of an individual and overly internalized spirituality that smacks of the self-help, "spiritual, not religious" philosophy that is so popular today.

A SACRAMENTAL APPROACH

That being said, my proposal for an ecclesiological model will be shown through a particular lens and aspect of the church: the sacraments. In what follows I will trace through the rites of confession, baptism, and the Eucharist. I have chosen this approach because it is evident to me that the sacraments are instruments by which the Spirit: (1) unites us to Christ and his body (the church); (2) transforms and shapes our identity; and (3) stabilizes our identity through the changes which occur over time. It is important to note here, briefly, that while I am using the NT language of "church" and "sacrament,"[2] this does not exclude those people prior to the formulation of the "church." The church throughout Scripture simply refers to the people of God and this is how I use the language here. That being said, while the language of "church" may be anachronistic to periods prior to the NT, the concept is not. In fact, as we will see through the survey of the sacraments, the ecclesiological rites all have corresponding OT events and tie into the corporate memory of all of God's people.

I have also chosen these particular sacraments due to their regular occurrence together throughout Scripture. For instance, we see in the Exodus narrative a baptismal text in the people's walking through the Red Sea (Exod 14), a confessional text in Moses's song (Exod 15), a eucharistic text in both the institution of Passover (Exod 12) and the promise of manna (Exod 16). We can see a similar theme in Joshua. The crossing of the Jordan River is a baptismal text (Josh 3–4), a eucharistic text can be seen in the celebration of Passover in Josh 5:10, and confession is seen in both the Rahab narrative (Josh 2) and Joshua's confession of lordship to the commander of the Lord's army (Josh 5:13–15). Finally, we also see the three together in Matt 14, where Jesus feeds the five thousand after breaking the bread in a way that is strikingly similar to the Last Supper (Matt

---

2. While the term *sacrament* is not strictly a NT term, it comes from the NT Greek term μυστήριον. The Latin term *sacramentum* was used to translate the Greek term which was used by Paul to refer to the hiddenness of Christ and his work before the incarnation (Eph 3:1–13).

14:19; 26:26), a story which is immediately followed by Peter's walking on water toward Jesus wherein he confesses Jesus as "Lord."[3]

Definition of Sacrament

The Sacraments

Having outlined the goals and method of this chapter, it is necessary first to offer a definition of the term *sacrament*. The sacraments have been the source of much controversy and division within the church and at many different levels. Not only do the Roman Catholic, Eastern Orthodox, and Protestant traditions disagree on what practices should be considered a sacrament, but an understanding of the word and the nature of a sacrament is hardly accepted universally. Therefore, it is important to think through an understanding of what makes an act or church rite sacramental. The words of Gerald Sittser offer us a helpful way forward in thinking through what a sacrament is or does:

> The sacraments are a source of genuine spiritual life and an objective means of grace. The tangible, concrete, material nature of the sacraments reminds us of the reality of Christ's saving work. The sacraments join the spiritual and material together into a seamless whole, just as the incarnation does. They are windows that allow us to gaze into another world and receive the grace that pours from that world into ours. . . . The Bible does not tell us *how* the sacraments actually communicate grace, only *that* they do. It is all a mystery.[4]

While this statement moves us forward in offering a framework, there are some necessary clarifications. First, the grace of the sacraments is not a salvific grace. Thus, one who is unable to partake in the sacraments can still speak of their justification and regeneration. Second, the sacrament is not the agent of grace. "Sacraments are the occasions, rather than the cause, of grace, which God alone causes."[5] Finally, it is helpful to highlight

---

3. There are other places in Scripture where I believe these three sacraments can be seen together, such as in the order of temple worship, the baptism of Jesus, as well as in the crucifixion of Jesus. However, I believe the examples I have shown are sufficient to make the case that throughout Scripture, these three sacraments are commonly seen hand in hand . . . in hand.

4. Sittser, *Water from a Deep Well*, 144, 160 (emphasis original).

5. Warrykow, "Sacraments in Thirteenth Century Theology," 222.

Sittser's incarnational point. The belief that a material object can occasion such grace and be joined with the spiritual is anchored in the incarnation. German theologians refer to Christ as the *Ursakrament* or "primordial sacrament" to speak of this Christological anchor of a sacramental theology.[6]

While Sittser's words are instructive, I will admit that they can hardly be described as a definition. We are still in need of a more concise statement that highlights the necessary elements of a rite for it to be considered sacramental. I believe Marc Cortez provides such a statement when he says that a sacrament is "a *unique* and *necessary* occasion in which *God acts* on his people in such a way as to *effect* their real transformation by making himself *present* to his people."[7] It is his definition made up of the five principles of uniqueness, necessity, divine agency, efficacy, and presence that I will work with as we move forward in discussing confession, baptism, and Eucharist.

Sacramental Ontology

Before moving on to a detailed look at the three sacraments and how they form identity, it is necessary to think through another way in which we might talk about "sacrament." There is a way that we might discuss sacramentality in a more general sense through which all of creation can be seen as relating sacramentally to the Creator, what Hans Boersma calls a "sacramental ontology."[8] The sacramental ontology is the more precise way of understanding what we saw earlier in Charles Taylor's discussion of an enchanted or porous world and self. Such an understanding sees the whole world as a mystery in that there are "realities behind the appearances," which we all take in by way of our senses throughout the world around us. Thus, a sacramental ontology simply refers to an ontology whereby "the created order [is] more than an external or nominal symbol. Instead it [is] a sign (*signum*) that point[s] to *and* participat[es] in a greater reality (*res*)."[9]

---

6. See Sonderegger, "Christ the *Ursakrament*," 111–23.

7. Cortez, "Who Invited the Baptist?," 205 (emphasis added). It is important to note that Cortez clarifies the necessity as well, "Most affirm that they [sacraments] cannot be strictly necessary since we have to allow for those circumstances where someone becomes a Christian without access to the sacraments. Yet we should be able to acknowledge those exceptional circumstances while maintaining that the sacraments are not optional for normal Christian living" (204).

8. See Boersma, *Heavenly Participation*; and *Nouvelle Théologie and Sacramental Ontology*.

9. Boersma, *Heavenly Participation*, 21, 23–24.

Why should we believe this? Boersma rightly points to passages such as Paul's message to the Areopagus where he states, "for 'In him we live and move and have our being'; as even some of your own poets have said, 'For we are indeed his offspring'" (Acts 17:28) and Paul's letter to Colossae where he writes, "And he is before all things, and in him all things hold together" (Col 1:17).[10]

Now, this does not take away from the particular, ecclesiological sacraments which we are discussing here. The sacraments of the church are still unique ways in which God participates with his church through his holy presence, as we will see, but there is a mysterious way in which all of creation participates in God. The particular aspect of God's creation that will be my focus here is time. In what way does time—in the sequential or successive moments understanding of time that we have—participate in a sacramental ontology?

It seems that it is this sacramental ontology and view of time that is in view in Scripture when two or more events can be seen as happening contemporaneously (e.g., sacrifice of Isaac and crucifixion of Jesus).[11] That being said, what I want to offer here is a way of understanding and seeing the practice of the sacraments (confession, baptism, and the Eucharist) as participating in an understanding of time within a sacramental ontology. I will seek to show a way in which God uses these sacraments to draw us into participation with our glorified selves, thereby stabilizing and grounding our identity in that future reality. Such a grounding will provide a way for our identity to be something that can be truly spoken about in concrete terms yet without the cost of downplaying those narratively indexed aspects of our identity as entirely secondary or non-essential.

BAPTISM

Baptism as Unifying

"For in one Spirit we were all baptized into one body—Jews or Greeks, slaves or free—and all were made to drink of one Spirit" (1 Cor 12:13).

---

10. Boersma, *Heavenly Participation*, 24. See also Isa 6:3 and Eph 1:23. Romans 1:19–20 seems to point in this direction as well.

11. See Taylor, *Secular Age*, 55. In fact, I believe it is this sacramentology that could be behind those arcane NT passages that seem to understand OT narratives as mysteriously happening in concurrence with later events (e.g., Matt 2:15 citing Hos 11:1, or 1 Cor 10:4 citing Exod 17:6).

These words speak to the entrance into the body of Christ which baptism brings. Baptism does more than just mark entrance and unity with the church, but it does not do less. Paul states elsewhere, in Eph 4:1–6:

> I therefore, a prisoner for the Lord, urge you to walk in a manner worthy of the calling to which you have been called, with all humility and gentleness, with patience, bearing with one another in love, eager to maintain the unity of the Spirit in the bond of peace. There is one body and one Spirit—just as you were called to the one hope that belongs to your call—one Lord, one faith, one baptism, one God and Father of all, who is over all and through all and in all.

Paul states that baptism is the entrance into and unifying to the body of all believers everywhere; baptism is an instrument by which God will "unite all things in him [Christ], things in heaven and things on earth" (Eph 1:10). "Baptism possesses such force as to make us one."[12] This truth occurs not just on the occasion of our own baptism. When another is baptized, we all celebrate the newness of life graciously given to the baptized. Our family grows, and we are drawn into another time of celebration together, all focused on the one thing bound by the unity that the Spirit brings because we all share in the "one baptism." As I will discuss more later, in my tradition (Anglican) and others, the faithful are reminded of this during baptisms when the priest uses an aspergillum to sprinkle the faithful with water from the baptismal font. We share in one baptism. However, I am not so naive as to be unaware that, at this point, the many differences in how churches baptize are glaringly obvious and may raise questions about the unifying nature of baptism. To this, Wolfgang Musculus, a theologian of the Reformation, has much to say that is worth quoting at length:

> Baptism is initiation and consecration in the name of the Father, the Son and the Holy Spirit, and it is incorporation into the church and the communion of saints. This is why there is not one baptism for one person and another for another, but all are baptized in the same way. Therefore, since we are all set apart by one and the same baptism and not by different ones, we are reminded that the harmony and unanimity of the church is maintained by the oneness of this sacrament. . . . It may however be asked how baptism can be one when Christ and the apostles, and later others who were baptized by the apostles at Christ's command, were baptized with John's baptism, if John's baptism and Christ's are not the same.

---

12. Calvin, *Galatians, Ephesians, Philippians*, 269.

Furthermore, how can baptism be one when it has three elements to it, water, fire and blood? Likewise, how can even the baptism of water alone, which the churches have practiced since the time of the apostles, be one, when some people give the Eucharist to newly baptized infants while others withhold it from them, when some baptize adults only, and others also baptize infants, when some immerse three times and others only once, when some immerse and others sprinkle, when some strip the baby naked and others only uncover its head, when some baptize with exorcisms, wax, salt, oil and spit, while others dispense with all that and use only water? Given such variety, how can we say that there is only one baptism in the church? My answer is that the unity of baptism is not located in the circumstances of the ministers baptizing nor of those being baptized, or in rites and external ceremonies, but in the substance, that is to say, in the name of him into whom we are baptized, the one God who is Father, Son and Holy Spirit.... The baptism of fire and blood does not involve another sacramental baptism, which is what the apostle is talking about here.[13]

This beautiful commentary brings our attention to the fuller degree of unity and oneness that the apostle Paul mentions in this passage of Ephesians: that is, the unity of the Triune God and the unity of his church, the Spirit-empowered body of Christ. This is the reality that baptism speaks to. Phillip Cary says it well when he comments on the article of the Nicene Creed which is drawn from this passage in Ephesians, "There is only one baptism because there is one holy Catholic Church throughout the world based on the faith taught by the apostles.... The one church has one faith because it has only the one Lord in whom to believe and be baptized." Cary continues, "It is the same baptism wherever it is the same Lord—so it is one baptism, not a different baptism in different churches, as if different congregations of the one Body of Christ each had a different head."[14] Cary, as does Musculus, astutely recognizes and notes that the one baptism is a matter of the unity of the one *body* that is necessarily under the one *head*, Christ. This is the true importance of recognizing the unity which baptism brings.

That is, baptism is marked by unity, not just of the church and its members to one another. It is also an event that is unified to the Trinity. Jesus, at his ascension, says to baptize "in the name of Father, Son and Holy Spirit" (Matt 28:19). In baptism, the Spirit draws us into Christ and reconciles us

---

13. Wolfgang Musculus, *Commentary on Ephesians*, cited in Bray, *Galatians, Ephesians*, 332–33.

14. Cary, *Nicene Creed*, 200.

to the Father. The baptism of Jesus gives us a glimpse of that truth. At Jesus' baptism, the Spirit descends like a dove, and the voice of the Father declares Jesus' sonship (Matt 3:13–17). Hilary of Poitiers (315–367), in commenting on this passage, says:

> As these events happened with Christ, we should likewise know that following the waters of baptism, the Holy Spirit comes upon us from the gates of heaven, imbuing us with the anointing of heavenly glory. We become the sons of God by the adoption expressed through the Father's voice. These actual events prefigured an image of the mysteries established for us.[15]

Thus, baptism is a Trinitarian event whereby we are reconciled to the Triune God and brought into unity with all of God's children.

Baptism as Identity Forming

Baptism as an event of identity transformation is not particularly novel. It is seen throughout passages such as Rom 6 and Col 2, where Paul links baptism with the language of putting off the old man and putting on the new. It can be seen most clearly in Col 2:11, whereby Paul connects baptism to the rite of circumcision. However, it is not just the fleshly circumcision of the Abrahamic covenant to which this speaks; it is also the circumcision of the heart, which is spoken of in the Law and Prophets.[16] This is important because Ezekiel connects the circumcision to the gift of the Spirit, which will be poured out onto God's people, giving them new life and a new heart via a circumcision made without human hands (Ezek 11:19; 36:26). All these things symbolize and signify new life (heart, spirit, death, burial, and resurrection) and therefore a new identity.

We also see the language of new life in the context of baptism in 1 Peter. Though the only explicit reference to baptism is found in 3:21, Peter does tie baptism to the resurrection of Christ. Furthermore, there is much baptismal and new life/birth language throughout the letter. In fact, some scholars have sought to argue that the context of the entire letter is that of a baptismal homily or rite.[17] While such a context is unlikely, the case can

---

15. Hilary of Poitiers, *Commentary on Matthew*, 53.

16. See Lev 26:41; Deut 10:16; Jer 4:4, 9:26; and Ezek 44:7–9.

17. Morales, *Bible and Baptism*, 157–58n2, citing F. L. Cross, *1 Peter: A Paschal Liturgy* (London: Mowbray, 1954); and Oscar S. Brooks, "1 Peter 3:21—The Clue to the Literary Structure of the Epistle" *NovT* 16 (1974) 290–305.

still be made that the letter holds the new life of baptism in context in much more than just the pericope surrounding the explicit mention. Isaac Augustine Morales, OP, makes such a case for the benediction of 1:3, "Blessed be the God and Father of our Lord Jesus Christ! According to his great mercy, he has caused us to be born again to a living hope through the resurrection of Jesus Christ from the dead."[18] Though Peter makes no explicit connection between baptism and new life/birth, it is a connection made elsewhere in Scripture. Not only is the case made in OT passages that foreshadow the sacrament (see below), but Paul speaks of a new self within a baptismal context in Eph 4, as we saw above, as well as the more explicit connection in the famous baptism passage of Rom 6. In addition, Peter ties being born again in 1:3 with the resurrection of Christ, just as he ties baptism with the resurrection in 3:21. Therefore, it seems likely that Peter would consider baptism as the moment of new life and new identity.

However, the connection between baptism and identity is not only clear in passages within the New Testament that speak of water baptism. It seems clear that the OT stories, which were a shadow of the future sacrament of the church, were linked to new life and new identity. One particularly notable instance is the story of Moses and the Israelites crossing the Red Sea and being liberated from the captivity and enslavement of the Egyptians. In the story, we see a picture of God's people entering the water and crossing through safely on the other side. Meanwhile, it is the Egyptians (their oppressor, their old life, the sin of their past) that are buried in the waters. On the other side of the waters is where a covenant is made with God, and they are given a new life, a new identity.

A little later, we see a similar story take place with the next generation as they come out of their extended wilderness wandering. Joshua has now taken the place of leadership and is leading the people into the promised land after forty years. In order to make it into the promised land, they must cross through the Jordan River. The Lord performs yet another miraculous feat by standing the water up in a heap, allowing the people to cross over on dry land. It is here that we see a few details that guide the reader into something of a new baptismal identity reading of the text.

First, we are given a strange detail about the waters heaping up at a city named "Adam." Comments on this text usually just recognize this as an historical detail for the purpose of showing what a miraculous feat this is since most scholars place the city of Adam approximately eighteen miles away.

18. Morales, *Bible and Baptism*, 160–62.

PART 3 | A SACRAMENTAL IDENTITY

However, there seems to be another meaning here, related to its echoes of the Exodus text of the Red Sea crossing, which Paul clearly states is a baptismal text in 1 Cor 10:1–4. It seems to me that the city of Adam also refers to the first man, Adam, who is consistently used throughout Scripture as a reference to the sinfulness of man. Baptism is a matter of putting to death the old man on the cross of Christ and putting on the new man through the resurrection of Christ. Strangely, we don't find this reading in the fathers either, who were ready to recognize the shared name of Joshua and Jesus as pointing toward Joshua as a type of Christ who would ultimately lead his people into the promised land. However, they seem to skip over the detail of the waters heaping up over the city of Adam, the city of man, as the people pass through on dry ground, leaving their old lives of wandering in the wilderness and exile behind.

Further, Joshua is commanded to gather twelve stones from their side of the river and build a monument on the dry land within the riverbed where the waters will eventually come down and bury it in the water. They will also build a memorial on the other side with stones gathered from the river to remember what the Lord did that day. The memorial signifies the death and burial of an old life and the creation of new life through the waters of the Jordan as God had done with the generation before them through the Red Sea.

While it seems clear from Scripture that baptism shapes identity, what place does the church body play in baptism's formation of identity? First and foremost, I believe accountability is a way that the communal, ecclesial element of baptism shapes one's identity. When you are making a covenant pledge to identify with something that is accompanied by a lifestyle change, accountability is necessary. For instance, one might claim and identify as a vegan, however the only thing that keeps that person accountable to the lifestyle and identification change is to publicly identify as such to those with whom you live life closely. Otherwise, there is no meaning to the individual's change—or lack thereof. Therefore, a baptism alone, even with just the pastor or priest, lacks substance as an identity claim due to the lack of encouragement and accountability from those who surround the baptized in the community. When the individual is tempted to resurrect the old self and live/identify with the old self, who is there to remind them of the death and new life that has come from the waters of baptism?[19]

---

19. My statement here assumes the position that something of a death and new life truly takes place in and through baptism contra the view that baptism simply commemorates

SACRAMENTAL IDENTITY

Further, I believe the story of Jesus healing the man born blind in John 9 gives us a perfect example of how social factors play into the identity transformation that baptism brings. In this famous healing narrative, there is a man who was born blind and is healed by Jesus in a rather unusual way. After Jesus rubs mud (made up of dirt and spit) on the man's eyes, he is told to wash in the pool of Siloam. The man comes back miraculously healed. Some of the early church fathers believed this to be a baptism text. Ambrose says:

> His making clay and anointing the eyes of the blind was intended to signify to us that the Same Who made man of clay, restored him to health by anointing with clay, and to signify also that this flesh of our clay must receive the light of eternal life by the Sacrament of Baptism. . . . Let Christ wash you that you may see. Come to Baptism, the time itself is at hand, make haste and come that you may say, *I went, and washed, and I received sight*; that you may also say, *whereas I was blind, now I see*, that you may say, as that man on whom light was poured said, *the night is far spent, the day is at hand*.[20]

What is also interesting about this passage from Ambrose is that he relates this text to the spiritual sight that we receive in baptism. Taking this interpretive approach to the washing in Siloam and the healing which occurs gives us another set of lenses by which we can view the narrative following the healing event.

In the remainder of the story, we are told of the changes which occur in the man's life and his identity as a result of the healing. In fact, this portion of the story takes up double the amount of space as the actual healing event itself (thirty-four verses in contrast to the seventeen verses of the healing event). The first aspect of this identity transformation is in the fact that people genuinely questioned whether the healed man was truly the same person as the man who had been born blind and whom they saw as a beggar (vv. 8–10). Now, while the questions they are asking are in reference to the numerical identity of this person, there is another element at play when we recognize the social factors behind the people speaking with the man who they thought was a beggar, one who had been seen as a social

---

the new life that we already have via our confession of faith. As a defense of my position is outside of the purview of this project, I believe it suffices to simply mention this difference as I do not believe the memorial position makes any substantial changes to what I have in mind here.

20. Ambrose, "Letter 80.6" (emphasis original).

outcast prior to his healing. The healing changed his social standing. The other identity factor that comes into play is in the beginning of the narrative when the disciples ask about the sinfulness of the man or his parents which led to his being born blind. The man was originally thought of as a sinner. However, "by the end of the narrative the man thought to be born in sin is a disciple of Jesus."[21]

What this narrative as a baptismal text teaches us is that baptism into discipleship transforms our identity. Not just in the way of being spiritually blind to being spiritually sighted, but also in the way that we relate to the outside world. It changes our self-conceptions, others' conceptions of us, and our self-expression. Our old self is put to death and our new self is brought to life in baptism, through the waters of new life and healing which union with Christ alone can offer. However, union with the body of Christ, the church, comes with union with Christ. You cannot take Christ and leave the church behind. This ecclesial community is then what informs and gives rich texture to our new identity. It is our difference and that of the other individuals in the community; it is our "I" and their "Thou" and the natural inverse that interpret and give meaning to this new identity.

Baptism as Stabilizing

In what way does the sacramentality of time affect the sacramental participation of the baptismal event with past and future events in a manner that stabilizes our identity? First, it is important to look at an important moment in scriptural history with which Paul sees baptism as having a sacramental union: the crucifixion, burial, and resurrection of Jesus. In Rom 6, Paul says, "Do you not know that all of us who have been baptized into Christ Jesus were baptized into his death? We were buried therefore with him by baptism into death, in order that, just as Christ was raised from the dead by the glory of the Father, we too might walk in newness of life" (vv. 3–4). Therefore, our baptism is a death of the old life and a resurrection into a new life in which we might walk.

However, the resurrection that Paul speaks of is not only the spiritual resurrection we partake in now. It speaks also of a future resurrection. Throughout 1 Cor 15, Paul argues for a coming bodily resurrection on the basis that Jesus received a bodily resurrection: "For if the dead are not raised, not even Christ has been raised. . . . But in fact, Christ has been

21. Fox, *Disability and the Way of Jesus*, 137.

raised from the dead, the firstfruits of those who have fallen asleep" (vv. 16, 20). Therefore, what Paul is looking toward in Rom 6 is not just the resurrection that comes to believers by the Holy Spirit in baptism, but also the future bodily resurrection of the dead that will come by the Holy Spirit. What this means is that baptism is an event that looks toward the future event of our resurrection into glory. These events could be said to happen contemporaneously in "higher time."[22]

What we see here is that baptism, and as I will argue is true of the rest of the sacraments, is a matter of both remembrance and anticipation. This necessarily means that in the present, it is also a matter of participation. This can be seen in the very liturgy of the church.[23] As one walks into the nave, they pass the baptismal font. This is for the express purpose of reminding the faithful of their baptism as they enter, as it is the sacrament of baptism that is the initiatory rite into the church. It is also custom for one to stop at the font, dip their fingers in the water, and cross themselves upon entering the nave as a way of participating bodily in that reminder. It is important to remember that, at this moment, we are, at once, remembering our baptism—which involves a remembrance of who we once were—and participating in our life as the baptized, as we anticipate not just the resurrection but also the Eucharist, which is a present or participatory resurrectional reality. The same is true as we exit the nave at the end of the liturgy. We dip at the font and cross ourselves as a reminder of the fact that we are the baptized, and it is by the power and grace of our baptism that we are able to go and live a resurrection life or, as the post-communion prayer of the eucharistic liturgy of the *BCP* says it, "so to assist us with thy grace, that we may continue in that holy fellowship, and do all such good works as thou hast prepared for us to walk in."[24]

The liturgy speaks to and reminds us of the fact that baptism is not just an event, but a way of life. This new life only comes by the power and

---

22. Taylor, *Secular Age*, 54-59.

23. I should reiterate here that I speak from my Anglican tradition, which is anything but universal. However, there is much that is rooted in the ancient catholic tradition, and it is these roots that I do my best to reflect on here.

24. Bray and Keane, *1662 Book of Common Prayer*, 265. The ACNA 2019 *BCP* preserves this prayer most closely in its "Anglican Standard Text." However, I prefer the language of the "Renewed Ancient Text" rite, "And now, Father, send us out to do the work you have given us to do, to love and serve you as faithful witnesses of Christ our Lord." We see the same thrust of vocation in both rites, but it is in the ancient text that we see something of what that vocation is all about, that is to be witnesses of the resurrected Christ, which is done by living a life of those who have been raised from the dead.

grace of the Triune God, which he gives us at baptism, but we are to live that baptismal identity forever. The title of Kevin J. Adams's book says perfectly that we are *Living under Water*. In his book, he explores through story and Scripture the answer to a question he asks early on about what it might look like if we understood that baptism was "the deepest part of our identity, the central, guiding reality that defines our lives?" Adams rightly recognizes throughout his book that identity and baptism are about story. "Baptism initiates Christians into an alternate story offering an inherited identity, a sense of belonging."[25] He continues later, "God directs, acts, and produces this story. We simply receive it as a kind of identity—a baptismal identity." The language of inheritance is useful here. Through baptism, we inherit God's story into our own. The story our lives are telling and which our identity speaks of is brought into God's story. Our story is Christ's story of death and resurrection. The story of our death and resurrection is different from others, and we bring our own story and identity as we come into God's story. We don't sacrifice authenticity or our identity, but our identity *is* given new meaning. Furthermore, the problems of an ever-changing and unstable identity grounded in our own isolated stories with an unknown end are stabilized by the story of unchanging God.

Our baptism brings stability to our identity in the midst of the changes which have occurred in the past and the changes which will occur in the future. In baptism and our inheritance of the story of God and Christ's death and resurrection, our identity is in sacramental participation with our stable and truest self of our resurrected and glorified future.

THE EUCHARIST

Eucharist as Unifying

It is Paul's words in 1 Cor 11:17–34 to which we are most indebted for our theological understanding of the Eucharist. Paul is addressing the sinful and divisive ways the Corinthians were partaking in the meal during their gathering. The primary problem, it seems, is that they have turned the *Lord's* Supper, an occasion to come together in unity as the body of Christ, to instead simply divide over conventional social differences of rank and status and their own meals. Thus, Paul is able to say, "When you come together it is not for the better but for the worse" (17:1). The problem with

---

25. Adams, *Living under Water*, 23.

this division is that it humiliates people in the community and misses the point of this practice instituted by Christ at the Last Supper. As Saint John Chrysostom noted in his homilies on the epistle, "The Corinthians were disgracing themselves by turning the Lord's Supper into a private meal and thus depriving it of its greatest prerogative. The Lord's Supper ought to be common to all because it is the Master's, whose property does not belong to one servant or to another but ought to be shared by all together."[26]

What we learn from this passage and Chrysostom's comments is that one of the primary purposes of the Eucharist is the unification of the body of Christ. The purpose of unity in the body is further shown in Eph 2:13–16:

> But now in Christ Jesus you who once were far off have been brought near by the blood of Christ. For he himself is our peace, who has made us both one and has broken down in his flesh the dividing wall of hostility by abolishing the law of commandments expressed in ordinances, that he might create in himself one new man in place of the two, so making peace, and might reconcile us both to God in one body through the cross, thereby killing the hostility.

Christ's death made such unity possible; thus, the eucharistic meal in remembrance of Christ's sacrifice is taken in vain when taken in division. Furthermore, 1 Cor 10:16–17 says, "The cup of blessing that we bless, is it not a participation in the blood of Christ? The bread that we break, is it not a participation in the body of Christ? Because there is one bread, we who are many are one body, for we all partake of the one bread." These passages seem to understand ecclesial unity as the ultimate goal of the sacrament.[27] Henri de Lubac argued that "the Eucharist corresponds to the Church as cause to effect, as means to end, as sign to reality."[28] The Eucharist sacramentally participates in the broken body of Jesus to unite the ecclesial body of Christ. Or stated more succinctly, "The Eucharist makes the Church."[29] I am in full agreement with the *Catechism of the Catholic Church* here, which states, "Those who receive the Eucharist are united more closely to Christ. Through it Christ unites them to all the faithful in one body—the Church.

---

26. John Chrysostom, *Homilies on the Epistles of Paul to the Corinthians* 27.4, cited in Bray, *1–2 Corinthians*, 111.

27. Boersma, *Heavenly Participation*, 115.

28. de Lubac, *Corpus Mysticum*, 13.

29. Cessario, *Seven Sacraments of the Catholic Church*, 211.

PART 3 | A SACRAMENTAL IDENTITY

Communion renews, strengthens, and deepens this incorporation into the Church, already achieved by Baptism."[30]

It is important to note here that the same question asked above regarding baptism and the many different beliefs or understandings of what happens at the Eucharist could be asked here. In what way can we truly understand the Eucharist as unifying when the sacrament has, in many ways, been one of the most divisive matters within the church across the many traditions/denominations? Certain traditions have a closed table disallowing any who have not been baptized and catechized within their tradition from taking Holy Communion in their churches. Therefore, in the quote from the Catholic Catechism above, I agree with the words but have a different understanding of their meaning. While the Roman Catholic Church (RCC) believes such unity is true for those who receive the body and blood of Christ, they do not believe that other Christians outside of the Roman Catholic faith have received the Holy Eucharist. However, despite such views, it is still my belief that wherever one truly receives the body and blood of Christ in the Holy Eucharist, they are drawn into unity with all the faithful, with the whole body of Christ. Paul is clear on this when he says, "The cup of blessing that we bless, is it not a participation in the blood of Christ? The bread that we break, is it not a participation in the body of Christ? Because there is one bread, we who are many are one body, for we all partake of the one bread" (1 Cor 10:16–17).

The issue in this apparent division within the body of Christ is that it focuses on historical realities. It is on this fact that Orthodox theologian Paul L. Gavrilyuk rightly notes, "In order to appreciate the degree of unity already shared by all Christians, one needs to attend to the christological and eschatological dimensions of the sacraments."[31] As I argued about baptism above, the Eucharist, too, participates sacramentally with eschatological realities. "Thus, the function of the Eucharist cannot be limited to the validation of an already existing unity. As an eschatological sign, the Eucharist has the potential to relativize all forms of existing human alienation; it is a purification of the fallen forms of unity (tribal, national, racial, political, and so on) that go against the believers' new life in Christ."[32] Despite what it may seem here, Gavrilyuk is not denying the importance of historical or even embodied unity and difference. As a faithful Orthodox

---

30. CCC no. 1396.
31. Gavrilyuk, "Eschatological Dimension of Sacramental Unity," 175.
32. Gavrilyuk, "Eschatological Dimension of Sacramental Unity," 176–77.

theologian, he would share a similar "closed table" sentiment to that of the RCC seen above. However, Gavrilyuk does recognize the need to relativize such historical matters of unity and difference in light of the great eschatological and kingdom realities in which the sacraments participate. He is worth quoting at length on this matter:

> To the extent to which baptism and Eucharist connect the believers with Christ and render them participants in the kingdom of God, partial *intercommunion is already a reality*. While such a conclusion seems inescapable, this reality is often passed over in silence, preoccupied as we are by our continuing differences. . . . It is important to acknowledge the eschatological reality of intercommunion before addressing the no less significant social, historical, and psychological realities of our divisions as well as our enduring theological differences. In baptism and Eucharist we are already partially eschatologically united, despite being historically divided. My distinction between the historical and eschatological dimensions of church unity does not intend to relegate the eschatological dimension to the nebulous sphere of the non-historical. On the contrary, the eschatological dimension stands for the divine action that breaks into the confines of history in the sacramental life of the church.[33]

In other words, the historical realities are important and true, but it is in the Eucharist (which is an historical reality in itself) that the eternal and eschatological realities of the kingdom break into these divisions and allow the church to participate in the full unity of the body of Christ. "Eucharistic communion anticipates the perfect union into which the faithful will be drawn in the eschaton."[34]

Eucharist as Identity Forming

If the goal of the Eucharist is to unite the body of Christ across all social, economic, and ethnic lines (as 1 Cor 11 and Eph 2 show), then in what way does the sacrament and its unifying goal shape one's identity? As I have argued above, social distinctions and classes were (and still are) shaping elements of one's self and one's own and others' conception of it. However, in eucharistic and ecclesial unity, it is not that we part with the diversity—as if

33. Gavrilyuk, "Eschatological Dimension of Sacramental Unity," 177.
34. Gavrilyuk, "Eschatological Dimension of Sacramental Unity," 178.

that is even possible in any real sense—we are not to segregate over it. Said another way, Christ has broken down the dividing wall of hostility (Eph 2:13–14), but that does not mean that the historical and embodied truths over which we often divide have been taken away.

This is a particularly relevant message to the church today and the issues that it faces. On one level, we can see ourselves in this passage as the church wrestles with questions concerning cultural and ethnic diversity in churches and unity and disunity. The Table of the Lord brings us all together in unity and can and should form our identity as individuals who celebrate such cultural and ethnic diversity as we truly image the eschatological vision of Rev 7:9–17. Indeed, this is part of that eschatological unity to which Gavrilyuk refers. On another level, we can also see how the Eucharist brings the church together in an ecumenical unity (the other aspect of that eschatological unity). While there may be a breadth and depth of difference within different Christian traditions on how we understand and practice the sacrament, the table still brings the universal church together in unity as we celebrate that "there is one body and one Spirit—just as you were called to the one hope that belongs to your call—one Lord, one faith, one baptism, one God and Father of all, who is over all and through all and in all" (Eph 4:4–6).[35] Despite the differences in church traditions on the proper understanding of the sacrament, its purposes, proper methods of participating in the sacrament, etc., it is still true that we are all taking the one bread and the one cup and remembering the same sacrifice of the one Lord, Jesus.

Therefore, the table of the Lord reminds us of the unity we share with the church because of the body of Christ. Tom Greggs says it the best in his recent work *Dogmatic Ecclesiology* when he says:

> This ongoing enactment of symbolic corporate identity (in which the whole church symbolizes that it is one because the church shares in one bread) is an ongoing commemoration of the single most important identity any individual possesses. This is the identity she possesses not primarily in and of herself but only *in solidum* in the community of the body of Christ . . . . The identity which Holy Communion repeatedly affirms is the identity the

---

35. I am not so naive as to think that this sacrament always brings external unity. This, in fact, is rarely ever the case. Division within the church often comes to a head in difference over the sacraments; however, in spiritual fact unity also comes to the fore within the practice of the sacraments. Again, see the points made above by Paul L. Gavrilyuk. This unity through the sacraments is the theme of the beautiful collection of essays in Kalantzis and Cortez, *Come, Let Us Eat Together*.

SACRAMENTAL IDENTITY

believer possesses in the community of those in communion with Christ and thereby one another.[36]

That is, the practice of the Lord's Supper celebrates our unity with Christ as we participate in the real presence of Christ through the bread and cup. However, it also brings us into unity with the *ecclesial* body of Christ, which was brought about by the broken *physical* body of Christ. It is this unity that becomes the most important identity marker for humanity as it points toward and gives us a taste of that identity for which we were made. Greggs continues:

> The community takes the form of its identity from this relationality towards God and other which becomes more fundamental than the individual's own identity in herself: in coming in communion with one another into symbolic communion with Christ, the believer is enacting (by the event of the act of the Holy Spirit) what it means to be united in Christ to one another. She therefore now has an individual identity which is radically relativized by the new identity—in which all individual identities now subsist—she receives in Christ.[37]

The key point in this is that the person's individual identity is not eradicated or even subsumed, as though the individual no longer exists in any meaningful way. Rather, that individual's identity is relativized and grounded upon their communion with God and the church through the Eucharist. It is hardly coincidental that after Paul drives home the point of unity within the Corinthian church (1 Cor 11), he follows up in chapter 12 with a teaching about the beauty and necessity of diversity within individuals.[38] Gordon Fee highlights this tightly knit argument between these two chapters:

> With this image [the body of Christ] Paul makes essentially two points: (a) Underlying the imagery is necessity of unity. . . . Whether Jew or Greek, slave or free, they are one in Christ through the Spirit. . . . God has so arranged the body that all members are essential to one another. (b) But his greater concern with this imagery is the concomitant necessity of diversity.[39]

---

36. Greggs, *Dogmatic Ecclesiology*, 226.
37. Greggs, *Dogmatic Ecclesiology*, 226–27.
38. Paul does the same thing in Rom 12, which follows a discussion on the grafting in of the gentiles to the people of God in Rom 11.
39. Fee, *First Epistle to the Corinthians*, 19–20.

PART 3 | A SACRAMENTAL IDENTITY

The Eucharist is an important identity-forming event, for it interprets and reshapes our own individual identity as it brings us into unity with Christ and his body. However, it is, in its very purpose, a communal event. First Corinthians teaches us how the sacrament is to be formed around the unifying event of the cross of Christ, whose body was broken and divided for the sake of the spiritual body of Christ (the church) that would be unified to each other and God by its atoning work. This unity thereby radically changes our perception of each other and ourselves.

Eucharist as Stabilizing

Finally, we look to the Eucharist as a means of inviting us into eschatological participation and stabilizing our identity. A cursory reading of the Gospels' accounts of the Last Supper will attune readers to the link between the table of the Lord and the Passover, which is inaugurated in Exod 12–13 (see Matt 26:17–29; Mark 14:12–25; Luke 22:7–23). In the Gospel accounts themselves, we are alerted to an event that is understood in sacramental time, for the supper is understood to be taking place almost simultaneously with the Passover meal. This is why Jesus can view his body as the unleavened bread and his blood as the blood of the paschal lamb, which was placed on the doorposts (Exod 12:3–7).[40] That being said, our participation in the Eucharist is a time when we are invited into a simultaneity of the Passover, the Last Supper, and the sacrifice of Christ on the cross.

Our mysterious, contemporaneous participation in these events does not end with that of the past. It extends into the future as it did for the disciples eating the Passover meal with Jesus. We are clued into this by Jesus' statement in Matt 26:29 (and parallels in Mark 14:25, Luke 22:18), "I tell you I will not drink again of this fruit of the vine until that day when I drink it new with you in my Father's kingdom." Jesus is referring to "the kingdom

---

40. While there is some debate on whether the OT allusion here in the Gospel accounts is to Exod 12 or to Exod 24, it seems to me that there is an obvious connection to the lamb in chapter 12. This can be seen in the fact that (1) the Synoptics give an explicit time marker of it being the day when they sacrifice the lambs, and (2) they seem to intentionally omit the presence of a sacrificed lamb at the meal. This is because Jesus is that sacrificial lamb whose blood is "a sign for you, on the houses where you are" (Exod 12:13). This does not mean that there is not an allusion to Exod 24—the grammatical allusion seems hard to miss—but this allusion does not negate the glaring material allusion to Exod 12.

of God in its consummate manifestation,"[41] at which time we will "rejoice and exult and give him the glory, for the marriage of the Lamb has come, and his Bride has made herself ready" (Rev 19:7). At the wedding of the Bride (the church) and the Lamb (see Eph 5:22–33) we will celebrate with "the marriage supper of the Lamb" (Rev 19:9; see also Matt 25:10). Apringius of Beja commented on Rev 19 in his *Tractate on the Apocalypse* saying:

> Who are those who have been invited to the feast of the Lamb, unless those to whom it is said: "I will not drink from this fruit of the vine until I will drink it new with you in the kingdom of my Father who is in heaven." . . . This is to drink the new cup, to prepare the new bodies of those being raised, to keep a new joy, and to repay the sincere righteousness of a true faith. These are the blessed who are prepared for this feast and for this repast.[42]

Indeed, the Eucharist not only points us back to Christ as the paschal lamb, sacrificed and broken for us, but is also future hope for the day when he will be the Lamb who is our—the church's/the bride's—bridegroom where he will drink of the vine once again in celebration of our being clothed in glory and unity.[43]

Scripture has made it clear that Christ's body and blood are present in the bread and wine of the Passover meal and that Christ is the paschal Lamb of God. John the Evangelist tells of the Baptist's pronouncement of Christ at his baptism, "The next day he saw Jesus coming toward him, and said, 'Behold, the Lamb of God, who takes away the sin of the world!'" (John 1:29). The Baptist declares this of Jesus again in verse 36. Paul makes it even more explicit in his first letter to the Corinthians when he says, "For Christ, our Passover lamb, has been sacrificed" (1 Cor 5:7). These declarations firm up the statement of Christ himself at the Last Supper when he told the disciples as he broke bread and shared the cup that "this is my body" and "this is my blood" in Matt 26:26–29 as we saw above.

Though controversy surrounds the following point, this is why the church has always seen and enacted an element of sacrifice in her eucharistic liturgy. This is not because the Eucharist is seen as a re-sacrifice of Christ, as many have supposed that such a sacrificial view believes, but because it is believed that through higher time or sacramental time, the Eucharist

---

41. Waters, *Lord's Supper as the Sign*, 91.

42. Cited in Weinrich, *Revelation*, 302–3.

43. For more on this, see Pitre, *Jesus the Bridegroom*; and Vickers, "Lord's Supper," 313–40.

participates in the singular sacrifice of Christ once for all. This truth already begins to show the Eucharist's participation in eternity. However, the fathers made it much clearer by showing how the eucharistic liturgy was a participation in the heavenly liturgy, participation with Christ's mediating priestly presence before the Father. French Catholic priest and patristic scholar Jean Daniélou, SJ, shows the ways in which the early fathers were saturated with this in the sacramental works. Commenting on the works of Saint Ambrose, Saint Cyril of Alexandria, Theodore of Mopsuestia, and Saint Chrysostom, he writes, "As the altar is the figure of Christ perpetually offering Himself to the Father in the heavenly sanctuary, so the deacons represent the angels who surround this heavenly liturgy. From this it is clear that the eucharistic sacrifice is the sacrament of the heavenly sacrifice. As it is Christ Who offers Himself under the symbol of the altar, so the angels are really present in the background of the visible liturgy."[44] Thus, the Eucharist participates sacramentally with the past and the future into eternity.

This is also seen in the "Memorial Acclimation" of some eucharistic rites. Though it is said in different ways throughout different traditions, it speaks of the same mystery in all of them. It is a mystery of hope and speaks to the past, present, and future of that faith in which we all put our hope. I cite the version with which I am most familiar, which is found in rite two of the *BCP 2019*:

> [Celebrant:] Therefore we proclaim the mystery of faith:
> *Celebrant and People*
> **Christ has died.**
> **Christ is risen.**
> **Christ will come again.**[45]

It is this mystery in which we participate and which we proclaim not just with our words but in our very actions each week in the Eucharist.

As I sought to show in the section on baptism above, what this means for our identity is stability throughout the changes that occur over time. The thing that both models of identity, which were explored earlier, suffer from is the issue of speaking to the temporal elements of identity, which are difficult to navigate. Changes to oneself and their identity throughout time are natural and impossible to avoid (in fact, such avoidance should not even be desirable), but to find one's identity entirely in those changes

---

44. Daniélou, *Bible and the Liturgy*, 131.
45. Anglican Church, *Book of Common Prayer* (2019), 133.

and identifying with every change to be authentic misses a fundamental element of identity and self.[46] However, to entirely ignore these differences and changes to find one's identity in something that is common to all human creatures is to not only be dishonest in a fundamental truth of human difference and identity but also ignore the beauty and importance of God's creativity in his diverse and unique creation of human beings.

This eternal participation of the Eucharist speaks two truths simultaneously: (1) we are sinners in need of a savior, and it is our sin that brought Christ to the cross, yet (2) we have been washed clean by the water and blood that poured from Christ's side on the cross.[47] This second truth is spoken of in Rev 19:7–8, "'Let us rejoice and exult and give him the glory, for the marriage of the Lamb has come, and his Bride has made herself ready; it was granted her to clothe herself with fine linen, bright and pure'—for the fine linen is the righteous deeds of the saints." We, the Bride, are clothed in white, bright and pure. And yet, before coming to the altar, we confess our sins. These truths are held in tension in the sacraments. It is the stability of this identity that is at once true and present and also one that we are coming into that holds stable the ever-changing nature of our complex identity as a whole. We find hope in the immutable, atemporal, and eternal Triune God for the disorienting nature of our mutable identity. This is done as we rightly remember the past by presently holding onto hope for the future in the sacraments, which tell the story of God's redemptive work throughout time.

---

46. Using such language of authenticity to describe following the changes of fleeting emotions, desires, or changes in one's self-perception and understanding is quite misleading. It seems to me to tell a story of an ulterior motive from those who encourage such an ideology, but an investigation of this kind would be a different project altogether.

47. It is common to mingle water with the wine in the chalice when preparing the elements for the Eucharist. This signifies two things: Christ's divine and human nature and the water and blood that poured forth from Christ's side after the soldiers pierced Jesus' side with the spear. It is interesting to note that even this truth of Christ's pierced side recalls the opened side of Adam from which his bride Eve was created as it points to the creation of Christ's bride, the church. Thus, even in this simple act, we signify our participation in the marriage supper of the Lamb.

PART 3 | A SACRAMENTAL IDENTITY

CONFESSION

Excursus: Confession as Sacrament

Traditionally the practice of confession has been claimed as a sacrament only by Roman Catholic and Eastern Orthodox doctrine,[48] along with six and five other sacraments, respectively. Though Luther defended the sacramentality of the rite,[49] Protestants have largely denied the practice as sacramental despite their emphasis on the importance and place of confession as a rite of the church. While offering a solution to the debate would require an entire thesis on its own, for my purposes here it is simply necessary to show that confession meets the five criteria of the definition offered above.

First, we must show how confession might be seen as an act in which God is the primary agent. When we understand confession as a rite which consists of both the confession of sins and of God's lordship, Paul makes the divine agency quite clear. In 1 Cor 12:3, Paul states, "No one can say 'Jesus is Lord' except in the Holy Spirit." The verse could hardly be clearer: It is impossible for anyone to make a confession of Jesus' lordship without the divine agency of the Holy Spirit undergirding this action. Further, within the immediate context of the verse, it is not just a confession of lordship that is in view, but also a confession of past sin. "It means that turning from their past blindness is made possible only by the reception of the Spirit."[50]

Next, it will be helpful to cover efficacy and necessity together. For these two principles it is helpful to look to two different places in Scripture: Prov 28:13, which says, "Whoever conceals his transgressions will not prosper, but he who confesses and forsakes them will obtain mercy," and 1 John 1:9, which states, "If we confess our sins, he is faithful and just to forgive us our sins and to cleanse us from all unrighteousness." Within these verses we can see both that it is necessary to confess sin and that confession truly does bring forgiveness. Again, it is important to note the divine agency of confession and that it is therefore not a meritorious act. However, Paul Hinlicky is still right when he says, "Forgiveness cannot be received apart from the acknowledgement of sin."[51]

---

48. Some Lutheran communions practice confession as a sacrament, but this is not universally observed as such.

49. See Luther, *Babylonian Captivity of the Church*, 4.1–19. See especially 4.1–2.

50. Garland, *1 Corinthians*, 572.

51. Cited in McCall, *Against God and Nature*, 360–61.

Finally, uniqueness and presence are admittedly more challenging to show. I believe the uniqueness of confession as "distinct from other ways in which God works efficaciously in the world"[52] can be seen as somewhat self-evident in the way that it draws us closer to God through vulnerability and honesty regarding our need for Christ. It also highlights the Creator/creature distinction and brings about the truth that John the Baptist spoke, "He must increase, but I must decrease" (John 3:30). I believe the principle of presence is similar in that it is in our recognition that only Christ who can forgive sins that we must know that it is truly he and his voice who are present when a Christian brother or sister tells us that we are forgiven. That is, we know that Christ gave authority to his children to forgive sins (John 20:23), but that authority and power is still Christ's. So, when we speak to one another "your sins are forgiven," we do not truly speak those efficacious words, but Christ through us.

Confession as Unifying

The final point made above regarding presence highlights that, in Scripture, confession is to be made in the presence of and to others. "And if he has committed sins, he will be forgiven. Therefore, confess your sins to one another" (Jas 5:15–16). This has been seen in Roman Catholic doctrine as something exclusively practiced with a priest due to their understanding of the OT priestly role as well as the way they understand the use of πρεσβύτερος in verse 14. However, Protestants have traditionally read this passage as a command to confess sins to one another and understood the priestly role as something that has shifted in light of Christ's work, as we see in Peter's words when he calls the church a "holy" and "royal" priesthood (1 Pet 2:5, 9). Thus, it seems that confession is not just done quietly and directly to God in isolation from others, it should also be practiced one to another.[53]

The point of confession to one another is important because of the way that the Spirit uses confession to bring unity to the community of the church. Dietrich Bonhoeffer emphasized this in his book *Life Together*, a

---

52. Cortez, "Who Invited the Baptist?," 204.

53. There is certainly a Scriptural precedent set for confession to be done in both ways. Matthew 6:5–15 gives us Jesus' model of prayer which involves praying alone (v. 6) and confessing sinfulness and asking for forgiveness (v. 12). However, I believe that it could be argued that the prayer also assumes confession one to another in verses 12, 14–15 where we are told to forgive others, which would require confession, at some level.

PART 3 | A SACRAMENTAL IDENTITY

book which he wrote while teaching in an underground seminary in Germany. Here in this book, which is centered on the importance of life in Christian community, he writes:

> In confession the break-through to community takes place. Sin demands to have a man by himself. It withdraws him from the community.... Since the confession of sin is made in the presence of a Christian brother, the last stronghold of self-justification is abandoned.... The expressed, acknowledged sin has lost all its power ... It can no longer tear the fellowship asunder. Now the fellowship bears the sin of the brother. He is no longer alone with his evil for he has cast off his sin in confession and handed it over to God.[54]

It seems that, to Bonhoeffer, it is not simply bringing the sin to light and repentance that is so important but also one's removal from isolation and into the family of faith where we might bear one another's burdens (Gal 6:2). It is here that one is caught up in Christ's grace and mercy as his bearing of our sins on the cross is imaged by our brothers and sisters in their sacrificial bearing of our burdens and their restoration which they offer through Christ (Gal 6:1). Moreover, it is difficult to overlook the fact that, as confession to one another brings the body of Christ into communion and unity, Jesus' words in Matt 18:20 must be recalled, "For where two or three are gathered in my name, there I am among them."[55] Therefore, confession not only unifies us (the church) one to another, but through confession the Holy Spirit also brings us into participation with Christ and unifies us to the Father.

The church has long taught confession as an important practice within the community of believers[56] and not just to God alone. This is because of

---

54. Bonhoeffer, *Life Together*, 112–13.

55. Interestingly, these words close out Jesus' teaching on the restoration and forgiveness or rebuke of one who has sinned against you, wherein we are told that what is bound or loosed on earth so shall it be in heaven (Matt 18:18–19). This further establishes the precedence for confession of sins to one another in order for the forgiveness of Christ in heaven to be offered here on earth. This teaching also immediately precedes the parable of the unforgiving servant, the impetus of which is Peter's rather foolish question regarding how often one must forgive one's sin against them. Jesus' parable shows that the forgiveness which one offers is always grounded in the forgiveness which is first offered by God, through Christ and perfected by the Spirit.

56. This does not just speak to confession of sin, but in those cases I do not mean to prescribe a public declaration of sin to the whole of the church body at once. I simply mean that confession is something that should be practiced one to another within the

the way that it draws us out of isolation and into unity with one another and with God. *The Didache*, an early church writing dated somewhere between the late first century (at its earliest) and mid to late second century (at its latest), speaks of confession and repentance as important for coming together as the church. "You shall confess your offenses in church, and shall not come forward to your prayer with a bad conscience" (4:14). The author(s) continue, "And on the Lord's Day, after you have come together, break bread and offer the Eucharist, having first confessed your offences, so that your sacrifice may be pure. But let no one who has a quarrel with his neighbor join you until he is reconciled" (14:1–2).[57] These passages make clear that confession to one another in the community of the church was not only important but was necessary for the sake of partaking in the Eucharist. The note about the Eucharist is of particular importance, for the sacrament of the Lord's table is focused on the unity of the ecclesial body of Christ as it partakes in the eucharistic body of Christ within the elements. Therefore, the importance for confession prior to the Table of the Lord is its unifying effects so that the Eucharist is possible and not taken in vain.

Cyprian of Carthage (AD 200–258) makes a similar claim in *On the Lapsed* while commenting on 1 Cor 11:27:

> He threatens, moreover, the stubborn and froward, and denounces them, saying, "Whosoever eateth the bread or drinketh the cup of the Lord unworthily, is guilty of the body and blood of the Lord." All these warnings being scorned and contemned,—before their sin is expiated, before confession has been made of their crime, before their conscience has been purged by sacrifice and by the hand of the priest, before the offence of an angry and threatening Lord has been appeased, violence is done to His body and blood; and they sin now against their Lord more with their hand and mouth than when they denied their Lord. They think that that is peace which some with deceiving words are blazoning forth: that is not peace, but war; and he is not joined to the Church who is separated from the Gospel.[58]

These are strong words from a bishop who was controversial in his own time; however, Cyprian captures the weight of Paul's stern warning.

---

body of Christ in order to combat the division that can occur within the church through bitterness and resentment from unresolved trespasses.

57. Translation of these passages come from Glimm, "Didache or Teaching of the Twelve Apostles."

58. Foxe, *Ante-Nicene Fathers*, *De laps.* 15–16.

Cyprian also clearly recognizes the double meaning in Paul's use of the word "body" here in reference to Christ's body. The violence which is done to Christ's body and blood is done not only to the body and blood of Christ in which the bread and wine sacramentally participate but done to the body and blood of Christ's ecclesial body. To divide the ecclesial body is to, in a manner of speaking, divide Christ's physical body all over again. Christ died for the unity which the Corinthians refused to participate in by remaining in their unconfessed sins of prejudice. Such lack of confession and division lives in denial of Christ's lordship and does violence to his body.

Finally, before moving on to confession as identity forming, it is important to remember that confession speaks not just to confession of sin. Such a practice is important and one aspect of confession, but the practice also contains the element of confessing Christ's lordship. This can be public confessions of the faith within an ecclesial body such as the recitation of the Apostles' Creed. Confessions of this sort are an important way for the church to remain unified by focusing on those elements of the Christian faith to which we all agree. This not only brings local bodies into unity under Christ's headship, but it is also a way for the universal and invisible body to come together under Christ's headship beyond other doctrinal disagreements.

Confession as Identity Forming

Confession becomes an identity-forming event in two modes. First, the confession of Christ's lordship becomes a confession of false identities[59] and an acknowledgment of who we were truly created to be. Second, such confession as it unifies us to the church brings us into communion with the one true and eternal community which rightly forms our identity as the members of the church continually point us forward toward that true identity1—bearers of God's image.

False Identities and True Identity

Confession includes confession of false identities and brings us into accountability for these. It gives us an opportunity to repent for these and

---

59. By false identity I mean identities ascribed to others which go against that which God has said about them. It is my contention that we ascribe these false identities to others when we sin against them.

SACRAMENTAL IDENTITY

pledge ourselves to deny false identities and hold fast to the truth of who we are. Michael Ovey brilliantly discusses this in terms of Martin Buber's famous *I and Thou*.[60] In *The Feasts of Repentance*,[61] Ovey discusses idolatry as a false identity and a confusion of relations with God and others. This is where Ovey finds great use of the language of Martin Buber and the terms of "I-Thou" relations and "I-It." While both have value, to see our relations with others as an "I-It" relation is to see our communion with them in terms of an object that can be known and mastered. This also limits us from seeing ourselves as a "Thou" to the other. Not only does this limit relationships with others, but Buber also spoke of how this would lead to a swollen ego, which would consequently distort our relation to God.[62] Ovey discusses how this looks in postmodern thought wherein objective reality and knowledge of the world "as it really is" becomes inaccessible: "I seem to be saying that a Thou cannot meet me: all there is is my own 'I,' and the other cannot disclose him or herself to me; at any rate not as he or she really is. I may perceive others but not meet them as they are."[63] This is idolatry and false identity insofar as it misrepresents the nature of God and his personhood and distorts the Creator/creature relation.

Another way false identities are ascribed to others—and to God—is by sinning against them. To sin against another is to sin against a bearer of God's image. For instance, in Gen 9:6, God shows that the destruction of an image bearer makes murder such a grievous sin. Jesus seemingly doubles down on this by noting that one is liable to the same judgment for being angry with their brother as they are for murdering (Matt 5:21–22). From this, it seems reasonable to conclude that unforgiving anger against a brother is to, in some way, destroy an image bearer. It is to ascribe a false identity to them and mock them. Further, it is important to note that to mock an image of God is not only mocking the image but also God himself.[64]

---

60. Buber, *I and Thou*.

61. Ovey, *Feasts of Repentance*.

62. Buber, *Eclipse of God*.

63. Ovey, *Feasts of Repentance*, 79. Ovey's distinction of how these distorted relations look in modern and postmodern thought comes at the behest of postmodern critiques of the dangers noted by Buber and the "I-It" tendency. Whereas modernity places an emphasis on "I-It" relationships and the knowability of others, postmodernity denies such capabilities and instead turns the danger to this "I-only" relations or lack thereof.

64. This is what makes 1 Sam 5 and the story of the Dagon statue falling over face first (twice!) and breaking such a powerful warning to the people of Ashdod. This was not just a mockery of the statue but, because the statue bore the image of Dagon, it was to make

PART 3 | A SACRAMENTAL IDENTITY

We can now see where confession and repentance to our church family and God rightly order these relationships. In the church and in confession, we admit to the distorted view of God and our relation to him. Confession of sin against another also admits to our distorted views of each other. When we sin against another, we strip them of their most fundamental identity marker, that they are created in the *imago Dei*. Though no one can truly strip another of this fundamental truth, we ascribe to them a false identity in the first sense, thus affecting their own self-conception. Confession of our sin against others clothes them once again with their dignity as an image bearer. Perhaps such ascription of dignity is an aspect of the healing that Jas 5 is speaking of in relation to confession: "Therefore, confess your sins to one another and pray for one another, that you may be healed."

Ecclesial Formation

The second way that confession shapes our identity comes out of the first. In other words, confession also allows us to know and be known in relationship with others by way of vulnerably confessing our sinfulness and pride. This also draws us into deeper communion with God as our brothers and sisters in the church remind us of God's forgiveness in Christ, pray with us, and help bear our burden and shame, which often holds us back from moving closer into communion with God. This establishes our identity firmly in the ways we are known by God and others rather than some authentic self that can only be known by ourselves but never truly known or perceived by others. It shows that our true selves can only truly be known in the right relationships (i.e., "I-Thou" relationships) with others, who often know us better than we know ourselves, and God, who is the only one who truly knows us perfectly.

Some of this ecclesial formation can be seen above, where we looked at Saint Augustine's understanding of confession and identity, wherein he tied these two closely to friendship. I will not expand on this aspect a lot here, but it is important to note a few things regarding confession within an ecclesial context, particularly the confession of sin that takes place in the liturgy of the church, which further strengthens the point of unification, but also forms us as people and as a church.

In the liturgy of several Christian traditions, communal confession of sin is practiced before coming to the altar for the Holy Eucharist. Such a

---

a mockery of Dagon himself.

practice does much to form the identity of individuals within the body of Christ and forms us as the church corporately as well. First, this practice further unifies us as a church and moves us away from a culture of hyper- and expressive individualism. To confess our sins together as a body brings us together as we communally express our humble equality before God, something that "The Prayer of Humble Access" confirms just a little later in the liturgy of the Anglican tradition, "We are not worthy so much as to gather up the crumbs under your table; but you are the same Lord whose character is always to have mercy."[65] Furthermore, such examination of ourselves is what prepares our hearts for coming to the Table of the Lord, where ultimate unity is found (1 Cor 11:27–29). This ecclesial unity is what then becomes the foundation for our ecclesial formation. To make my point, I need to show an example of this communal confession. To do so, I quote the confessional prayers from the *BCP* 2019 Rite 1, followed by Rite 2:

> Almighty God, Father of our Lord Jesus Christ, maker and judge of us all:
> We acknowledge and lament our many sins and offenses, which we have committed by thought, word, and deed
> against your divine majesty,
> provoking most justly your righteous anger against us. We are deeply sorry for these our transgressions;
> the burden of them is more than we can bear. Have mercy upon us,
> Have mercy upon us, most merciful Father;
> for your Son our Lord Jesus Christ's sake,
> forgive us all that is past;
> and grant that we may evermore serve and please you in newness of life,
> to the honor and glory of your Name;
> through Jesus Christ our Lord. Amen.
>
> Most merciful God,
> we confess that we have sinned against you
> in thought, word, and deed,
> by what we have done, and by what we have left undone.
> We have not loved you with our whole heart; we have not loved our neighbors as ourselves.
> We are truly sorry and we humbly repent. For the sake of your Son Jesus Christ,
> have mercy on us and forgive us;

---

65. Anglican Church, *BCP* (2019), 135.

that we may delight in your will, and walk in your ways, to the glory of your Name. Amen.[66]

Notice the language: the prayers are said in the first-person plural, not the singular. Such a choice is purposeful. We confess as the church together, even as we state the things about ourselves that conceivably separate us from God, it does not change who we are fundamentally. We come together as the children of God, humbly confessing our sinfulness, yes, but also confessing our place in his family, a fundamental aspect of who we are because of our baptism. "For I am sure that neither death nor life, nor angels nor rulers, nor things present nor things to come, nor powers, nor height nor depth, nor anything else in all creation, will be able to separate us from the love of God in Christ Jesus our Lord" (Rom 8:38–39). A confession of sin made together as the unified body of Christ, through the grace of the sacrament of baptism, is not just a confession of actions done or left undone but a confession (and re-affirmation) of our identity.

Such a point deserves more elaboration. It may seem that the above point only confirms that our identity is in Christ and that confession is simply a place to remind ourselves and be reminded by God that this is true. It does not necessarily entail that our identity is found and formed in the actual sacrament of baptism. However, this is where a sacramental view of confession makes the difference. If you believe, as I do, that a mysterious or sacramental grace is received at the moment of confession and absolution, then my argument above takes on a stronger meaning wherein the confession and the subsequent forgiveness that is bestowed is an ontologically transformative grace which forms who we are and our own understanding of ourselves. Paul Louis Lehmann, in conversation with Karl Barth, says it well:

> Man exists altogether by the grace of God. When man is forgiven, he is forgiven *in toto* and *from moment to moment*. The consequence of the discontinuity between God and man is that God *forgives* man as the sheer miracle of his love and that when he forgives, man's whole existence is changed. . . . Forgiveness . . . is the paradox of a futuristic indicative, of a forgiveness that is present as a hope, as a promise, and which in spite of its being a promise is at the same time an event for the man to whom it comes. We have grace. Yes, but in no sense as a possession of our own.[67]

---

66. Anglican Church, *BCP* (2019), 112–13, 130.
67. Lehmann, cited in Coutts, *Shared Mercy*, 13 (emphasis original).

Confession forms us as it gives us a correct view of ourselves. That view is necessarily a nuanced one. The view does not exist on the foundation of what might be called either an under- or over-realized eschatology. As Lehmann says above, we *are* forgiven (*in toto*), but we are also being forgiven (*from moment to moment*). In the communal confession of the liturgy, in the sacrament, we also receive absolution, and it is there that we submit ourselves to Christ and the truths that are spoken of us in the sacrament. Recall Augustine's view on memory, the past, and the present. Confession is a matter of memory but with the right understanding of it through the passage of time and the view toward the future.

Confession as Stabilizing

As I mentioned above, I believe that a sacramental ontology, particularly a sacramental understanding of time, offers us a way of seeing the sacraments as an invitation to participate with our future, glorified selves. I have established that such an understanding of time is what allows Scripture to speak of two events in history happening contemporaneously. That being said, it is my contention that each of the three sacraments is an event that happens simultaneously with past and future events through the "higher" or "sacramental" time we discussed earlier. If this is true, then we have here a way of understanding the sacraments as stabilizing our present identity throughout the past changes that have occurred and the future changes that will occur toward our destiny as we are "conformed to the image of his [God's] son" (Rom 8:29).

Confession, on its surface, can be seen as containing a look at the past with a hope toward the future. We are presently confessing our past sins with a hope toward the ultimate reconciliation to God and his kingdom, which will be fully consummated in the future. However, this takes on a greater depth when we see confession as linked to idolatry in the above mentioned ways.

If confession is a matter of confession of idolatry, then we can link this to two extremely important events within Scripture. The first is that event wherein mankind was created in the image of God. Much work has been done on the image of God, which has noticed that the language in Genesis is akin to language within other ANE texts recounting the creation of idols and crafted images of other gods. In these ceremonies, the presence of the god was seen as coming into the image so that it might truly mark the presence of the god wherever it might be.[68] This is then what makes it such a grievous thing for mankind to create idols or images as it not only makes other things into an image of God that do not truly reflect or carry his presence, but it denies a core aspect of our created selves.

Therefore, in light of this understanding, we develop a greater understanding of what it means when Scripture tells us that Christ is the image of God (2 Cor 4:4; Col 1:15). He is the true image of God. Thus, we are later told that we are being conformed to the image of Jesus (Rom 8:29;[69] 1 Cor 15:49). Here, we see events that might take place contemporaneously through this sacramental time. Within the event of confession, we confess not only the ways in which we have created idols of other things but also that we have failed to be a proper image of God, as we were created to be. This gives a richer and more thoroughly canonical reading of Paul's telling us that we are a "new creation" (2 Cor 5:17). That is, we are newly created in the image of Christ, who is the true and perfect image of God.[70]

Yet, as we see in 1 Cor 15:49, "we shall bear the image of the man of heaven" in the future. Thus, the event of confession seems to be linked by "higher time" to the future event that will take place where "we will all stand before the judgment seat of God" and "every knee shall bow to me, and every tongue shall confess to God" (Rom 14:10, 11). Paul cites the words of the Lord here from Isa 45:23, which are spoken in a larger context of the nation's idolatry. Thus, confession is not only an identity-forming event in the ways we saw earlier, but it also is a means by which our identity is stabilized through time. As we presently confess, we sacramentally participate with our past, sinful selves and bow ourselves before God. However, we also participate in our final confession before the Lord when "the trumpet will sound, and the dead will be raised imperishable, and we shall be changed" (1 Cor 15:52).

---

68. See Cortez, *ReSourcing Theological Anthropology*, 99–129; Curtis, "Man as the Image of God"; Lints, *Identity and Idolatry*.

69. For an in depth look at this powerful phrase, see Jacob, *Conformed to the Image of His Son*.

70. At this point, an argument may be raised that a simple memorial understanding, whereby confession clearly points backward and forward to these events, is all that is necessary. However, seeing how such a view offers the metaphysical payout needed for the identity stabilizing I am looking for here is difficult. Thus, a sacramental view of time, in which the three events are truly present with each other in some way, offers a more robust metaphysic by which to understand the stabilization of our identity within our past, present, and future selves.

SACRAMENTAL IDENTITY

The sacraments are an instrument of the Holy Spirit's work to transform God's people, his church. Not only are they instruments that work toward our sanctification, but they change our self-conceptions and identity. The sacraments draw us into closer communion with the Trinity, and this changes us. However, the sacraments also draw us into the family of God: we are united together as the body of Christ. As we are united with the Divine other and the ecclesial other, we are drawn out of our isolated, individualistic self.

Whereas the authenticity model would argue that our identity is only truly found in this turn toward the self, the contrary is true. The outside world influences us. It is a cultural script—an external narrative—that this inward turn marks authenticity. The program shows itself to be self-defeating: to seek authenticity in the self is to have bought into a cultural script and to lose this version of individualistic authenticity already. Therefore, we are most authentically ourselves when we accept the influence that others have on us.

What greater "other" could there be than the transcendent Other who created us and knows us better than we could ever know ourselves? And yet, this transcendent Other is also immanent. In fact, our Creator came to us in the truly human person of Jesus, who then sent the Spirit so that we might be united with him. While the "in-Christ" model may stop here, believing that in this unity our identity is finally found, this is not the full picture. Our Creator is also present with us through the sacraments, and these sacraments draw us into unity with the ecclesial body of Christ: the corporeal extension of Christ's incarnation. Diverse, storied people form this ecclesial body and tell the story of the church and continue the story of God's redemptive plan. It is only together in our diversity—living authentically in the ways God made us—that we make up the body of Christ. Indeed, as the apostle Paul said, "If all were a single member, where would the body be?" (1 Cor 12:19). Thus, we find our true authentic selves in our union with Christ and his body. That is, as we unite our story with God's story we are able to see the story God has truly been telling with our lives all along.

7

Conclusion

In Eugene Peterson's famous "conversation" in spiritual reading, *Eat This Book*,[1] he notes two particularly important things about Scripture: (1) it is a story, and we cannot read it outside of its storied nature, and (2) we are called into that story, to participate in the storied nature of Scripture. It has been my goal to bear these things in mind throughout my work. We are people of the text. Whatever our understanding of identity (or anything for that matter), it must participate in the text of Scripture, that means it must participate in the story. Therefore, while my work has been that of information-based, systematic theology, I have sought to retain a narrative.

It has been my contention that both the authenticity model and the current/popular accounts of the "in-Christ" model of identity are, in one way or another, not storied enough. While the authenticity model boasts of its storied nature, it ultimately proposes a story of one. However, there is no story with only one character. Take, for instance, Robert Zemeckis's award-winning film *Cast Away*. The island-stranded Chuck Noland begins his journey on the island seemingly alone. He seeks solace and friendship in the memory of his girlfriend, Kelly Frears. At this point, the story feels as though it has come to a crashing halt. There is little to no dialogue, and the circumstances feel hopeless. It is only later, when Chuck's companion, Wilson, is created and enters the film, and Chuck is no longer alone, that the story can truly continue. In years of isolation, what gives his story meaning, what gives him hope and a sense of identity are those who are in the

---

1. Peterson, *Eat This Book*.

CONCLUSION

story with him.[2] The "in-Christ" model, however, often bypasses the storied nature of the individual as a subsidiary of our newfound union with Christ. Such a notion damages the storied nature of Scripture and God's invitation to join our story with his.[3] If our story is, in fact, a part of his story, then the narratively indexed aspects of ourselves cannot simply be covered over as if joining God's story acts as some sort of redaction over the script so far. No, our narratively indexed identity brings rich texture to God's story. When we tell our stories as a part of God's story, we act as witnesses to the richness of God's storytelling. His story is one filled with rich character development of many diverse, multifaceted characters all across God's global stage. This is why the authors of Scripture are so intent on telling us something of the past story of the characters they introduce. Paul's story as apostle is what it is because of our knowledge of him as the zealous Saul. The stories of the chosen disciples throughout the Gospels are brought to life because of our knowledge of them as fishermen and tax collectors.

That being said, when the paths of two plots meet, the characters of that plot cannot go unchanged. As God is immutable, it is only we who can change. However, that change is still shaped by the story and shape of that character so far. Who we see Saint Paul, the apostle to the gentiles, to be is surprising but not out of line with who we saw in the infamous Saul of Tarsus. God's story shapes our own when we come in contact with it through the church, by realigning it toward its creationally intended goal, not by papering over it. The problem with the common models of identity is their lack of attention not just to the storied nature of identity, but their misunderstanding of how (good) stories work.

The authenticity model falls deeply into the problem that James K. A. Smith discusses in *On the Road with Saint Augustine*: they see the road as home. It misses the importance of a *telos* in a story. In a story, the development of a character means something primarily when the story reaches its end, and we are able to put all the pieces together. Suddenly, we discover

---

2. Furthermore, Chuck Noland is time-obsessed, a major aspect of who he is as a person, a part of his identity. Yet, in isolation, this core part of him is not retained. Stranded, where the construct and illusion of clock time are shattered, he becomes more aware of those around him and permanently changes.

3. There is, in fact, some truth in the statement that God, as sovereign, is not so much inviting us to join our story with his—as though our story prior is somehow independent of his—as much as he is inviting us to recognize that our story is a part of his larger story. However, the beauty of God's story is that it is being told by many people in many different cultural contexts, geographical and social locations, and enacted by many different and diverse bodies.

PART 3 | A SACRAMENTAL IDENTITY

seemingly mundane moments in a character's plot were turning points. We realize that horrible decisions made were pivotal for the growth of the character to be who they needed to be by the very end. However, by the end of it all, it was the story overall that held and stabilized all of these things along the way, even if the end was not fully known or understood at the time; as Saint Augustine shows, the road is not home, it can't be, "Our hearts are restless" until they find rest in the author of the story himself. This is why the authenticity model falls into the problem of a lack of stability of identity throughout the changes that occur over time. There is no cohesive story or *telos* in which to ground our changing identity.

The "in-Christ" models that we have seen seemingly fail to realize the importance of the story by either erasing the narrative entirely or speaking of a prioritization of the divine story as though the stories told in the embodied particulars of people are not one and the same. What I mean by this is that it doesn't seem to recognize, again, that the narrative in the embodied life of people is the narrative of God. This is the way in which the "in-Christ" model can fail to answer the problems of change and stability. It isn't always honest about the ways in which our relationship with—our knowing and being known by—God changes throughout time due to the ever-changing realities of our embodied existence. How does our identity in Christ and our understanding of that identity change as we age, or if our bodies become disabled in some way, or as our social location changes the way we understand and interact with our racialized bodies? A faithful theological understanding of our identity must speak to these matters because these embodied realities are witnesses to God's creation and what God is doing in the world. This is attested to in the fact that God's ultimate self-revelation and the crux of God's story is found in the incarnation.

Theological anthropology dictates a Christologically centered anthropology in which we look at Jesus as the model of what it means to be human, which entails faithfully living out the embodied realities in which we were made and doing so "authentically." However, this doesn't require an inward turn; in fact, it requires the opposite. To live authentically as ourselves, we must be honest about the social location and relations in which we live, namely, the church. We must also bring our bodies into union with Christ and allow our bodies to worship and tell the story of God and our place in it. So, where do we find a scriptural (storied), theologically robust, model of personal identity? This is the question that I have set out to answer, and I have argued that it can be found in the sacraments. The sacraments are where we bring our whole bodies together as the church to tell the story of God and allow our whole selves to be formed into the people that God has made us to be. We are baptized into the community of God and the story itself and into the new identity out of which we will now live. We confess the ways in which we have sinned in our bodies—"in thought, word, and deed"[4]—and broken communion with God and others and misaligned our embodied lives from the story that God is telling. We are nourished in the Eucharist as we feed on the bread of life and are brought into unity with the body of Christ and participate in Christ's sacrifice for us and in the resurrection wherein Christ won the victory over death. Furthermore, as I argued above, these sacraments are where time, in some way, converges, and we are able to bring who we were into who we are in the present and participate in who God is making us to be.

---

4. *BCP*, 130.

Bibliography

Adams, Kevin J. *Living under Water: Baptism as a Way of Life*. Grand Rapids: Eerdmans, 2022.
Allen, Michael. "Toward Theological Theology: Tracing the Methodological Principles of John Webster." *Themelios* 41.2 (2016) 217–37.
Allison, Gregg. *Historical Theology: An Introduction to Christian Doctrine*. Grand Rapids: Zondervan Academic, 2011.
Ambrose. "Isaac, or the Soul (*De Isaac vel anima*)." In *Seven Exegetical Works*, translated by Michael P. McHugh, 9–68. Washington, DC: Catholic University of America Press, 2003.
———. "Letter 80.6." In *The Letters of Saint Ambrose*. Translated by H. Walford. Oxford: James Parker, 1881. https://www.gutenberg.org/files/58783/58783-h/58783-h.htm#b459a.
———. "The Mysteries." In *Theological and Dogmatic Works*, translated by Roy J. Deferrari, 5–28. Washington, DC: Catholic University of America Press, 2002.
Anglican Church of North America. *The Book of Common Prayer*. Huntington Beach, CA: Anglican Liturgy, 2019.
Assmann, Jan. *Cultural Memory and Early Civilization: Writing, Remembrance, and Political Imagination*. Cambridge: Cambridge University Press, 2011.
———. "Cultural Memory: Script, Recollection, and Political Identity in Early Civilizations." Translated by Ursula Ballin. *Historiography East & West* 1.2 (2003). 157–77.
Augustine. *Confessions*. Translated by Henry Chadwick. 1st ed. Oxford: Oxford University Press, 2009.
———. *Confessions*. Translated by R. S. Pine-Coffin. Harmondsworth, Middlesex, Engl: Penguin Classics, 1961.
———. *Confessions*. Edited by Roy Joseph Deferrari. Translated by Vernon J. Bourke. The Fathers of the Church 21. Washington, DC: Catholic University of America Press, 1953.
Bartholomew, Craig G., and Michael W. Goheen. *Christian Philosophy: A Systematic and Narrative Introduction*. Grand Rapids: Baker Academic, 2013.
Beale, G. K. *Colossians and Philemon*. Grand Rapids: Baker Academic, 2019.
———. *We Become What We Worship: A Biblical Theology of Idolatry*. Downers Grove, IL: IVP Academic, 2008.
Bellah, Robert N., et al., eds. *Habits of the Heart, with a New Preface: Individualism and Commitment in American Life*. Berkeley: University of California Press, 2007.
Benner, David G. *The Gift of Being Yourself: The Sacred Call to Self-Discovery*. Enlarged/expanded ed. Downers Grove, IL: InterVarsity, 2015.

BIBLIOGRAPHY

Bennett, David. *A War of Loves: The Unexpected Story of a Gay Activist Discovering Jesus.* Grand Rapids: Zondervan, 2018.

Billings, J. Todd. *Union with Christ: Reframing Theology and Ministry for the Church.* Grand Rapids: Baker Academic, 2011.

Black, J. A., et al. "Enki and Ninmah: Translation." *The Electronic Text Corpus of Sumerian Literature.* Oxford, 1998. http://www-etcsl.orient.ox.ac.uk/.

Boersma, Gerald P. "Ambrose: Baptismal Identity and Human Identity." In *Sources of the Christian Self*, edited by James M. Houston and Jens Zimmermann, 168–91. Grand Rapids: Eerdmans, 2018.

Boersma, Hans. *Embodiment and Virtue in Gregory of Nyssa: An Anagogical Approach.* Oxford: Oxford University Press, 2013.

———. *Heavenly Participation: The Weaving of a Sacramental Tapestry.* Grand Rapids: Eerdmans, 2011.

———. *Nouvelle Théologie and Sacramental Ontology: A Return to Mystery.* Oxford: Oxford University Press, 2013.

———. *Scripture as Real Presence: Sacramental Exegesis in the Early Church.* Grand Rapids: Baker Academic, 2018.

Boersma, Hans, and Matthew Levering, eds. *The Oxford Handbook of Sacramental Theology.* Oxford: Oxford University Press, 2018.

Bonhoeffer, Dietrich. *Life Together.* New York: HarperOne, 1978.

Bray, Gerald L., ed. *1–2 Corinthians.* 2nd ed. Ancient Christian Commentary on Scripture, New Testament 7. Downers Grove, IL: IVP Academic, 2006.

———, ed. *Galatians, Ephesians.* Reformation Commentary on Scripture, New Testament 10. Downers Grove, IL: IVP Academic, 2011.

Bray, Samuel L., and Drew Nathaniel Keane, eds. *The 1662 Book of Common Prayer: International Edition.* Downers Grove, IL: IVP Academic, 2021.

Brown, Jeannine K. "Metalepsis." In *Exploring Intertextuality: Diverse Strategies for New Testament Interpretation of Texts*, edited by B. J. Oropeza, 29–41. Eugene, OR: Cascade, 2016.

Brown, Peter. *Augustine of Hippo: A Biography.* 45th anniversary ed. Berkeley: University of California Press, 2013.

Buber, Martin. *Eclipse of God: Studies in the Relation between Religion and Philosophy.* Princeton: Princeton University Press, 2015.

———. *I and Thou.* Translated by Walter Kaufmann. New York: Touchstone, 1971.

Burk, Dennis R., and Heath B. Lambert. *Transforming Homosexuality: What the Bible Says about Sexual Orientation and Change.* Phillipsburg, NJ: P&R, 2015.

Calvin, John. *Calvin: Institutes of the Christian Religion.* Edited by John T. McNeill. Translated by Ford Lewis Battles. Louisville: Westminster John Knox, 1960.

———. *Galatians, Ephesians, Philippians, and Colossians.* Vol. 11, *Calvin's New Testament Commentaries.* Grand Rapids: Eerdmans, 1996.

Cary, Phillip. *The Nicene Creed: An Introduction.* Bellingham, WA: Lexham, 2023.

Cessario, Romanus. *The Seven Sacraments of the Catholic Church.* Grand Rapids: Baker Academic, 2023.

Chalmers, Aaron. *Exploring the Religion of Ancient Israel: Prophet, Priest, Sage and People.* Downers Grove, IL: IVP Academic, 2012.

Cicero. *On Moral Ends.* Edited by Julia Annas. Translated by Raphael Woolf. Cambridge: Cambridge University Press, 2001.

BIBLIOGRAPHY

Clements, Ronald E. *The World of Ancient Israel: Sociological, Anthropological and Political Perspectives*. Cambridge: Cambridge University Press, 1991.

Coakley, Sarah. *God, Sexuality, and the Self: An Essay "On The Trinity."* Cambridge: Cambridge University Press, 2013.

———. "The Eschatological Body: Gender, Transformation, and God." *Modern Theology* 16.1 (2000) 61–73.

Cohick, Lynn H. *Ephesians: A New Covenant Commentary*. Eugene, OR: Cascade, 2010.

Coles, Gregory. *Single, Gay, Christian: A Personal Journey of Faith and Sexual Identity*. InterVarsity, 2017.

Collins, Nate. *All But Invisible: Exploring Identity Questions at the Intersection of Faith, Gender, and Sexuality*. Grand Rapids: Zondervan, 2017.

Copleston, Frederick. *Modern Philosophy: From Descartes to Leibnitz*. New York: Image, 1993.

Cortez, Marc. "Nature, Grace, and Christological Ground." In *The Christian Doctrine of Humanity*, edited by Oliver D. Crisp and Fred Sanders, 23–40. Grand Rapids: Zondervan Academic, 2018.

———. *ReSourcing Theological Anthropology: A Constructive Account of Humanity in the Light of Christ*. Grand Rapids: Zondervan Academic, 2018.

———. "Who Invited the Baptist?" In *Come, Let Us Eat Together*, edited by George Kalantzis and Marc Cortez, 200–218. Downers Grove, IL: IVP Academic, 2018.

Coulmas, Florian. *Identity: A Very Short Introduction*. Oxford University Press, 2019.

Coutts, Jon. *A Shared Mercy: Karl Barth on Forgiveness and the Church*. Downers Grove, IL: IVP Academic, 2016.

Creamer, Deborah. "Finding God in Our Bodies: Theology from the Perspective of People with Disabilities, Part 1." *Journal of Religion in Disability and Rehabilitation* 2.1 (1991) 67–87.

Crisp, Oliver D., and Fred Sanders, eds. *The Christian Doctrine of Humanity: Explorations in Constructive Dogmatics*. Grand Rapids: Zondervan Academic, 2018.

Curtis, Edward M. "Image of God (OT)." In *The Anchor Bible Dictionary, Vol. 3: H-J*, edited by David Noel Freedman, 389-91. New York: Doubleday, 1992.

———. "Man as the Image of God in Genesis in the Light of Ancient Near Eastern Parallels." PhD diss., University of Pennsylvania, 1984.

Daniélou, Jean. *Bible and the Liturgy*. 1st edition. Notre Dame, IN: University of Notre Dame Press, 2002.

Davison, Andrew. *Participation in God*. Cambridge: Cambridge University Press, 2020.

———. *Why Sacraments?* Eugene, OR: Cascade, 2013.

DeFranza, Megan K. *Sex Difference in Christian Theology: Male, Female, and Intersex in the Image of God*. Grand Rapids: Eerdmans, 2015.

DeLashmutt, Michael W. "Paul Ricoeur at the Foot of the Cross: Narrative Identity and the Resurrection of the Body." *Modern Theology* 25.4 (2009) 589–616.

de Lubac, Henri. *Corpus Mysticum: The Eucharist and the Church in the Middle Ages*. Translated by Gemma Simmonds CJ. 1st ed. Notre Dame, IN: University of Notre Dame Press, 2007.

Dictionary.com. "Identity—Dictionary.Com's 2015 Word of the Year." *Dictionary.Com* (blog), Dec 8, 2015. https://www.dictionary.com/e/identity/.

Dieleman, Karen. *Religious Imaginaries: The Liturgical and Poetic Practices of Elizabeth Barrett Browning, Christina Rossetti, and Adelaide Procter*. Athens, OH: Ohio University Press, 2012.

Di Vito, Robert A. "Old Testament Anthropology and the Construction of Personal Identity." *Catholic Biblical Quarterly* 61.2 (1999) 217–38.
Dunn, James D. G. *The Epistles to the Colossians and to Philemon.* Grand Rapids: Eerdmans, 2014.
Dunson, Ben C. "All for One and One for All: Individual and Community in Paul and Epictetus." In *Paul and the Giants of Philosophy: Reading the Apostle in Greco-Roman Context*, 61–73. Downers Grove, IL: IVP Academic, 2019.
Eastman, Susan Grove. *Paul and the Person: Reframing Paul's Anthropology.* Grand Rapids: Eerdmans, 2017.
Eiesland, Nancy L. *The Disabled God: Toward a Liberatory Theology of Disability.* Nashville: Abingdon, 1994.
Emmert, Kevin P. *The Water and the Blood: How the Sacraments Shape Christian Identity.* Wheaton: Crossway, 2023.
Epictetus. *Discourses, Books I–II.* Translated by W. A. Oldfather. Loeb Classical Library. Cambridge, MA: Harvard University Press, 1925.
Esler, Philip Francis. "Paul and Stoicism: Romans 12 as a Test Case." *New Testament Studies* 50.1 (Jan 2004) 106–24.
Evans, C. Stephen. *A History of Western Philosophy: From the Pre-Socratics to Postmodernism.* Downers Grove, IL: IVP Academic, 2018.
Fee, Gordon D. *The First Epistle to the Corinthians.* Rev. ed. Grand Rapids: Eerdmans, 2014.
Ferguson, Everett. *Baptism in the Early Church: History, Theology, and Liturgy in the First Five Centuries.* Grand Rapids: Eerdmans, 2013.
———. *Church History, Volume One: From Christ to the Pre-Reformation: The Rise and Growth of the Church in Its Cultural, Intellectual, and Political Context.* 2nd ed. Grand Rapids: Zondervan Academic, 2013.
Fielder, Bronwyn, and Douglas Ezzy. *Lesbian, Gay, Bisexual and Transgender Christians: Queer Christians, Authentic Selves.* London: Bloomsbury Academic, 2017.
Fox, Bethany McKinney. *Disability and the Way of Jesus: Holistic Healing in the Gospels and the Church.* 1st ed. Downers Grove, IL: IVP Academic, 2019.
Foxe, A. Cleveland, et al. *Ante-Nicene Fathers.* Vol. 5. New York: Christian Literature, 1886.
Fox, Helen. *Their Highest Vocation: Social Justice and the Millennial Generation.* New York: Peter Lang, 2011.
Frame, John M. *A History of Western Philosophy and Theology.* Phillipsburg, NJ: P&R, 2015.
Freedman, David Noel, ed. *The Anchor Bible Dictionary, Vol. 1: A-C.* New Haven, CT: Yale University Press, 1992.
Garland, David E. *1 Corinthians.* Grand Rapids: Baker Academic, 2003.
Gavrilyuk, Paul L. "The Eschatological Dimension of Sacramental Unity." In *Come, Let Us Eat Together*, edited by George Kalantzis and Marc Cortez, 170–83. Downers Grove, IL: IVP Academic, 2018.
Gay, Peter. *The Enlightenment: The Rise of Modern Paganism.* New York: Norton, 1995.
Gilson, Rachel. *Born Again This Way: Coming Out, Coming to Faith, and What Comes Next.* Good Book, 2020.
Glimm, Francis X. "The Didache or Teaching of the Twelve Apostles." In *The Apostolic Fathers*, translated by Francis X. Glimm et al. Fathers of the Church 1. Washington, DC: Catholic University of America Press, 1947.

Greggs, Tom. *Dogmatic Ecclesiology: The Priestly Catholicity of the Church*. Grand Rapids: Baker Academic, 2019.

Grogan, G. W. "The Old Testament Concept of Solidarity in Hebrews." *Tyndale Bulletin* 49.1 (May 1998) 159–73.

Harrison, Nonna Verna. *God's Many-Splendored Image: Theological Anthropology for Christian Formation*. Grand Rapids: Baker Academic, 2010.

Harrison, Verna E. F. "Gender, Generation, and Virginity in Cappadocian Theology." *Journal of Theological Studies* 47.1 (1996) 38–68.

Hartke, Austen. *Transforming: The Bible and the Lives of Transgender Christians*. Louisville: Westminster John Knox, 2018.

Heidel, Alexander. *The Babylonian Genesis: The Story of Creation*. Chicago: University of Chicago Press, 1951.

Hilary of Poitiers. *Commentary on Matthew*. Translated by D. H. Williams. Washington, DC: Catholic University of America Press, 2013.

Hill, Wesley. *Washed and Waiting: Reflections on Christian Faithfulness and Homosexuality*. Enlarged ed. Grand Rapids: Zondervan, 2016.

Horne, Brian L. "Person as Confession: Augustine of Hippo." In *Persons, Divine and Human*, edited by Christoph Schwöbel and Colin E. Gunton, 65–73. Edinburgh: T. & T. Clark, 1991.

Houston, James M., and Jens Zimmermann, eds. *Sources of the Christian Self: A Cultural History of Christian Identity*. Grand Rapids: Eerdmans, 2018.

Jacob, Haley Goranson. *Conformed to the Image of His Son: Reconsidering Paul's Theology of Glory in Romans*. Downers Grove, IL: IVP Academic, 2018.

Jacobson, Rolf. "We Are Our Stories: Narrative Dimension of Human Identity and Its Implications for Christian Faith Formation." *Word and World* 34.2 (2014) 123–30.

Johnson, Dru. *Human Rites: The Power of Rituals, Habits, and Sacraments*. Grand Rapids: Eerdmans, 2019.

Kalantzis, George, and Marc Cortez, eds. *Come, Let Us Eat Together: Sacraments and Christian Unity*. Downers Grove, IL: IVP Academic, 2018.

Kant, Immanuel. "What Is Enlightenment?" In *The Philosophy of Kant*, edited and translated by Carl J. Friedrich, 132–39. New York: Rand House, 1949.

Kapic, Kelly M. *You're Only Human: How Your Limits Reflect God's Design and Why That's Good News*. Grand Rapids: Brazos, 2022.

Krieg, Laurie, and Matt Krieg. *An Impossible Marriage: What Our Mixed-Orientation Marriage Has Taught Us about Love and the Gospel*. Downers Grove, IL: InterVarsity, 2020.

Leary, Mark R., and June Price Tangney, eds. *Handbook of Self and Identity, Second Edition*. New York: Guilford, 2013.

Lehmann, Paul Louis. *Forgiveness: Decisive Issue in Protestant Thought*. New York: Harper & Brothers, 1940.

Lieu, Judith. *Neither Jew nor Greek? Constructing Early Christianity*. 2nd ed. London: T. & T. Clark, 2015.

Lints, Richard. *Identity and Idolatry: The Image of God and Its Inversion*. Downers Grove, IL: IVP Academic, 2015.

Ludlow, Elizabeth. *Christina Rossetti and the Bible: Waiting with the Saints*. London: Bloomsbury Academic, 2014.

———. "Christina Rossetti: Her Identity in the Communion of Saints." In *Sources of the Christian Self: A Cultural History of Christian Identity*, edited by James M. Houston and Jens Zimmermann, 543–53. Grand Rapids: Eerdmans, 2018.

Luther, Martin. *The Babylonian Captivity of the Church*. Translated by J. J. Schindel and C. M. Jacobs, in vol. 2 of Works of Martin Luther with Introductions and Notes. 6 vols. Philadelphia: A. J. Holman, 1915.

Macaskill, Grant. *Union with Christ in the New Testament*. Oxford: Oxford University Press, 2018.

Malina, Bruce J. "Who Are We? Who Are They? Who Am I? Who Are You (Sing.)? Explaining Identity, Social and Individual." *Annali Di Storia Dell'esegesi* 24.1 (Jan 2007) 103–9.

Martin, Luther H. "The Anti-Individualistic Ideology of Hellenistic Culture." *Numen* 41.2 (May 1994) 117–40.

Mathison, Keith A. "The Lord's Supper." In *Reformation Theology*, edited by Matthew Barrett, 644–46. Wheaton, IL: Crossway, 2017.

McAfee, Melonyce. "'Identity' Is the Dictionary.com Word of the Year." CNN, Dec 8, 2023. https://www.cnn.com/2015/12/08/living/word-of-the-year-dictionary-com-feat/index.html.

McCall, Thomas H. *Against God and Nature: The Doctrine of Sin*. Wheaton: Crossway, 2019.

McConville, J. Gordon. *Being Human in God's World: An Old Testament Theology of Humanity*. Grand Rapids: Baker Academic, 2018.

McGill, Jenny, ed. *The Self Examined: Christian Perspectives on Human Identity*. Abilene, TX: Abilene Christian University Press, 2018.

McGrath, Alister E. *Christian Theology Reader*. 2nd ed. Cambridge, MA: Wiley-Blackwell, 1996.

McKnight, Scot. *A Community Called Atonement*. Nashville: Abingdon, 2007.

———. *Five Things Biblical Scholars Wish Theologians Knew*. Downers Grove, IL: IVP Academic, 2021.

———. "I Am Church: Ecclesial Identity and the Apostle Paul." *Covenant Quarterly* 72.3–4 (Aug 2014) 217–32.

Meeks, Wayne A. "The Image of the Androgyne: Some Uses of a Symbol in Earliest Christianity." *History of Religions* 13.3 (1974) 165–208.

Mitchell, L. L. "Ambrosian Baptismal Rites." *Studia Liturgica* 1.4 (Dec 1, 1962) 241–53.

Moo, Douglas J. *The Letters to the Colossians and to Philemon*. Grand Rapids: Eerdmans, 2008.

Morales, Isaac Augustine. *The Bible and Baptism: The Fountain of Salvation*. CBTS. Grand Rapids, Michigan: Baker Academic, 2022.

Noble, Alan. *Disruptive Witness: Speaking Truth in a Distracted Age*. Downers Grove, IL: InterVarsity, 2018.

———. *You Are Not Your Own: Belonging to God in an Inhuman World*. Downers Grove, IL: InterVarsity, 2021.

O'Keefe, Tim. *Epicureanism*. Berkeley: University of California Press, 2009.

Oropeza, B. J., and Steve Moyise, eds. *Exploring Intertextuality: Diverse Strategies for New Testament Interpretation of Texts*. Eugene, OR: Cascade, 2016.

Osborne, Grant R. *Colossians and Philemon Verse by Verse*. Bellingham, WA: Lexham, 2016.

Ovey, Michael J. *The Feasts of Repentance: From Luke-Acts to Systematic and Pastoral Theology*. Downers Grove, IL: IVP Academic, 2019.

Oyserman, Daphna, et al. "Self, Self-Concept, and Identity." In *Handbook of Self and Identity*, edited by Mark R. Leary and June Price Tangney, 69–104. 2nd ed. New York: Guilford, 2012.

Paglia, Camille. *Vamps & Tramps: New Essays*. New York: Vintage, 1994.

Paige, Terence P. "Philosophy." In *Dictionary of Paul and His Letters*, edited by Gerald F. Hawthorne et al, 713–18. Downers Grove, IL: InterVarsity, 1993.

Pearcey, Nancy R. *Love Thy Body: Answering Hard Questions about Life and Sexuality*. Baker, 2019.

Perry, Jackie Hill. *Gay Girl, Good God: The Story of Who I Was, and Who God Has Always Been*. Nashville: B&H, 2018.

Peterson, Eugene H. *Eat This Book: A Conversation in the Art of Spiritual Reading*. Grand Rapids: Eerdmans, 2009.

———. *Practice Resurrection: A Conversation on Growing Up in Christ*. Grand Rapids: Eerdmans, 2013.

Peterson, Ryan S. "Created and Constructed Identities in Theological Anthropology." In *The Christian Doctrine of Humanity: Explorations in Constructive Dogmatics*, edited by Oliver D. Crisp and Fred Sanders, 124–43. Grand Rapids: Zondervan Academic, 2018.

———. *The Imago Dei as Human Identity: A Theological Interpretation*. 1st ed. Winona Lake, IN: Eisenbrauns, 2016.

Pitre, Brant. *Jesus the Bridegroom: The Greatest Love Story Ever Told*. New York: Image, 2018.

———. *Jesus and the Jewish Roots of the Eucharist: Unlocking the Secrets of the Last Supper*. New York: Image, 2016.

Pullen, Christopher. *Gay Identity, New Storytelling and the Media*. Basingstoke: Palgrave Macmillan, 2012.

Reinders, Hans S. *Receiving the Gift of Friendship: Profound Disability, Theological Anthropology, and Ethics*. Grand Rapids: Eerdmans, 2008.

Reynolds, Thomas E. *Vulnerable Communion: A Theology of Disability and Hospitality*. 1st ed. Grand Rapids: Brazos, 2008.

Ricoeur, Paul. *Time and Narrative, Volume 3*. Translated by Kathleen Blamey and David Pellauer. Chicago: University of Chicago Press, 1990.

Robinson, H. Wheeler. *The Christian Doctrine of Man*. London: Forgotten Books, 2015.

Rogerson, J. W. "Corporate Personality." In *The Anchor Bible Dictionary, Vol. 1: A-C*, edited by David Noel Freedman, 1156–57. New York: Doubleday, 1992.

———. "The Hebrew Conception of Corporate Personality: A Re-Examination." *Journal of Theological Studies* 21.1 (1970) 1–16.

Root, Andrew. *Faith Formation in a Secular Age: Responding to the Church's Obsession with Youthfulness*. Grand Rapids: Baker Academic, 2017.

Rosner, Brian S. *How to Find Yourself: Why Looking Inward Is Not the Answer*. Wheaton: Crossway, 2022.

———. *Known by God: A Biblical Theology of Personal Identity*. Grand Rapids: Zondervan Academic, 2017.

Rossetti, Christina. *The Complete Poems*. Edited by R. W. Crump. Reprint ed. New York: Penguin Classics, 2001.

———. *The Face of the Deep: A Devotional Commentary on the Apocalypse*. Whitefish, MT: Kessinger, 2008.

Schreiner, Thomas R., and Matthew R. Crawford, eds. *The Lord's Supper: Remembering and Proclaiming Christ until He Comes*. Nashville: B&H Academic, 2011.

Seneca. *Epistulae Morales ad Lucilium*. Translated by R. M. Gummere. Loeb Classical Library. Cambridge: Harvard University Press, 1917–25.

———. *Letters from a Stoic*. Translated by Robin Campbell. New York: Penguin Classics, 2015.

———. *Moral Essays*. Translated by John W. Basore. Loeb Classical Library. London: W. Heinemann, 1928–35.

Shapiro, Joseph P. *No Pity: People with Disabilities Forging a New Civil Rights Movement*. New York: Crown, 1994.

Shurley, Anna Katherine. *Pastoral Care and Intellectual Disability: A Person-Centered Approach*. Waco: Baylor University Press, 2017.

Shuve, Karl. *The Song of Songs and the Fashioning of Identity in Early Latin Christianity*. Oxford: Oxford University Press, 2016.

Sittser, Gerald L. *Water from a Deep Well: Christian Spirituality from Early Martyrs to Modern Missionaries*. Downers Grove, IL: InterVarsity, 2010.

Smith, James K. A. *Desiring the Kingdom: Worship, Worldview, and Cultural Formation*. Grand Rapids: Baker Academic, 2009.

———. *How (Not) to Be Secular: Reading Charles Taylor*. Grand Rapids: Eerdmans, 2014.

———. *Imagining the Kingdom: How Worship Works*. Grand Rapids: Baker Academic, 2013.

———. *On the Road with Saint Augustine: A Real-World Spirituality for Restless Hearts*. Grand Rapids: Brazos, 2023.

———. *You Are What You Love: The Spiritual Power of Habit*. Grand Rapids: Brazos, 2016.

Snodgrass, Klyne R. "Introduction to a Hermeneutics of Identity." *Bibliotheca Sacra* 168.669 (Jan 2011) 3–19.

———. "Pauline Perspectives on the Identity of a Pastor." *Bibliotheca Sacra* 168.672 (Oct 2011) 387–401.

———. "Paul's Focus on Identity." *Bibliotheca Sacra* 168.671 (Jul 2011) 259–73.

———. *Who God Says You Are: A Christian Understanding of Identity*. Grand Rapids: Eerdmans, 2018.

Solomon, Robert C. *Continental Philosophy since 1750: The Rise and Fall of the Self*. Oxford: Oxford University Press, 1988.

Sonderegger, Katherine. "Christ the *Ursakrament*." In *Come, Let Us Eat Together*, edited by George Kalantzis and Marc Cortez, 111–23. Downers Grove, IL: IVP Academic, 2018.

Stubbs, David L. *Table and Temple: The Christian Eucharist and Its Jewish Roots*. Grand Rapids: Eerdmans, 2020.

Swinton, John. *Becoming Friends of Time: Disability, Timefullness, and Gentle Discipleship*. Waco: Baylor University Press, 2018.

Taylor, Charles. *The Ethics of Authenticity*. Reprint ed. Cambridge: Harvard University Press, 2018.

———. *A Secular Age*. Reprint ed. Cambridge, MA: Belknap, 2018.

———. *Sources of the Self: The Making of the Modern Identity*. Cambridge: Harvard University Press, 1992.

Tennent, Timothy C. *Theology in the Context of World Christianity: How the Global Church Is Influencing the Way We Think about and Discuss Theology*. Grand Rapids: Zondervan Academic, 2007.
Thilly, Frank. "Locke's Relation to Descartes." *Philosophical Review* 9.6 (1900) 597–612.
Thompson, Marianne Meye. *Colossians and Philemon*. Grand Rapids: Eerdmans, 2005.
Thorsteinsson, Runar M. "Paul and Roman Stoicism: Romans 12 and Contemporary Stoic Ethics." *Journal for the Study of the New Testament* 29.2 (Dec 2006) 139–61.
Tran, Jonathan. *The Vietnam War and Theologies of Memory: Time and Eternity in the Far Country*. Malden, MA: Wiley-Blackwell, 2010.
Trueman, Carl R. *The Rise and Triumph of the Modern Self: Cultural Amnesia, Expressive Individualism, and the Road to Sexual Revolution*. Wheaton: Crossway, 2020.
———. *Strange New World: How Thinkers and Activists Redefined Identity and Sparked the Sexual Revolution*. Wheaton: Crossway, 2022.
Tucker, J. Brian, and John Koessler. *All Together Different: Upholding the Church's Unity While Honoring Our Individual Identities*. Chicago: Moody, 2018.
Twiss, Richard. *One Church Many Tribes*. Ventura, CA: Chosen, 2000.
———. *Rescuing the Gospel from the Cowboys: A Native American Expression of the Jesus Way*. Downers Grove, IL: InterVarsity, 2015.
U. S. Catholic Church. *Catechism of the Catholic Church: Complete and Updated*. Rev. ed. New York: Doubleday, 1995.
Vanhoozer, Kevin J. *Faith Speaking Understanding: Performing the Drama of Doctrine*. Louisville, KY: Westminster John Knox, 2014.
Vickers, Brian J. "The Lord's Supper: Celebrating the Past and Future in the Present." In *The Lord's Supper*, edited by Thomas R. Schreiner and Matthew R. Crawford, 313–40. Nashville: B&H Academic, 2010.
Volf, Miroslav. *After Our Likeness: The Church as the Image of the Trinity*. 1st ed. Grand Rapids: Eerdmans, 1997.
———. *The End of Memory: Remembering Rightly in a Violent World*. Grand Rapids: Eerdmans, 2021.
———. *Exclusion and Embrace, Revised and Updated: A Theological Exploration of Identity, Otherness, and Reconciliation*. Nashville: Abingdon, 2019.
Walls, Jerry L. *Heaven, Hell, and Purgatory: Rethinking the Things That Matter Most*. Grand Rapids: Brazos, 2015.
———. *Heaven: The Logic of Eternal Joy*. Oxford: Oxford University Press, 2002.
Walton, John H. *Genesis*. Grand Rapids: Zondervan Academic, 2001.
Walton, John H., et al. *The IVP Bible Background Commentary: Old Testament*. Downers Grove, IL: IVP Academic, 2000.
Walton, John H., and J. Harvey Walton. *The Lost World of the Torah: Law as Covenant and Wisdom in Ancient Context*. Downers Grove, IL: IVP Academic, 2019.
Warren, Tish Harrison. *Liturgy of the Ordinary: Sacred Practices in Everyday Life*. Downers Grove, IL: InterVarsity, 2019.
Warrykow, Joseph. "The Sacraments in Thirteenth Century Theology." In *The Oxford Handbook of Sacramental Theology*, edited by Hans Boersma and Matthew Levering, 218–34. Oxford: Oxford University Press, 2015.
Waters, Guy Prentiss. *The Lord's Supper as the Sign and Meal of the New Covenant*. SSBT. Wheaton: Crossway, 2019.
Wax, Trevin. *Eschatological Discipleship: Leading Christians to Understand Their Historical and Cultural Context*. Nashville: B&H Academic, 2018.

BIBLIOGRAPHY

Weinrich, William C., ed. *Revelation*. Ancient Christian Commentary on Scripture, New Testament 12. Downers Grove, IL: IVP Academic, 2005.

White, Vernon. *Identity*. London: SCM, 2002.

Williams, Rowan. *On Augustine*. London: Bloomsbury Continuum, 2016.

———. *Wound of Knowledge: Christian Spirituality from the New Testament to St. John of the Cross*. Cambridge: Cowley, 2003.

Yerushalmi, Yosef Hayim. *Zakhor: Jewish History and Jewish Memory*. Seattle: University of Washington, 2011.

Zizioulas, John D. *Being as Communion: Studies in Personhood and the Church*. Crestwood, NY: St. Vladimirs Seminary Press, 1997.

www.ingramcontent.com/pod-product-compliance
Lightning Source LLC
Chambersburg PA
CBHW051940160426
43198CB00013B/2238